WEAPON

THE PIAT

MATTHEW MOSS
Series Editor Martin Pegler

Illustrated by Adam Hook & Alan Gilliland

OSPREY PUBLISHING
Bloomsbury Publishing Plc
Kemp House, Chawley Park, Cumnor Hill, Oxford OX2 9PH, UK
1385 Broadway, 5th Floor, New York, NY 10018, USA
E-mail: info@ospreypublishing.com
www.ospreypublishing.com

OSPREY is a trademark of Osprey Publishing Ltd

First published in Great Britain in 2020

A catalogue record for this book is available from the British
Library.

ISBN: PB 9781472838131; eBook 9781472838124;
ePDF 9781472838148; XML 9781472838117

20 21 22 23 24   10 9 8 7 6 5 4 3 2 1

Index by Rob Munro
Typeset by PDQ Digital Media Solutions, Bungay, UK
Printed and bound in India by Replika Press Private Ltd.

To find out more about our authors and books visit
www.ospreypublishing.com. Here you will find extracts, author
interviews, details of forthcoming events and the option to sign
up for our newsletter.

Dedication

To Lauren, for all her support and encouragement.

Author's acknowledgements

Thank you to the many collections and institutions which were
kind enough to facilitate my research. Special thanks go to the
staff of the Royal Armouries Library, the archives at Nuffield
College, Teesside Archives, the Trustees of the Small Arms School
Corps Museum and the Ridgeway Military and Aviation
Research Group Historical Collection. I'd also like to express my
appreciation to the numerous institutions which have allowed the
use of images from their collections to illustrate the PIAT's
history. Thank you to my parents for all their support, and
thanks also to Richard Fisher, Neil Gibson and Jonathan Ware
for their assistance and to everyone who supported me and this
project, to literally 'bring up the PIAT!'

Front cover, above: This PIAT, part of the Royal Armouries'
collections, has an early-pattern A-frame monopod but also has a
straight butt and quadrant sights. An experimental adapter is
fitted in its bomb-support tray for firing practice rounds.
(© Royal Armouries PR.1551)
Front cover, below: A PIAT gunner of 1st Battalion, The Norfolk
Regiment, is pictured during the advance on Wanssum in the
Netherlands, 26 November 1944. (Sgt Laing/Imperial War
Museums via Getty Images)
Title-page photograph: A No. 2 (loader) of a PIAT team from
1st Battalion, The London Irish Rifles, loads a bomb into his
PIAT's bomb-support tray during a training exercise in Italy,
February 1945. Surrounding them are empty PIAT fuze
containers and projectile loading clips. (© IWM NA 22007)

Imperial War Museums Collections

Many of the photos in this book come from the huge collections
of IWM (Imperial War Museums) which cover all aspects of
conflict involving Britain and the Commonwealth since the start
of the twentieth century. These rich resources are available online
to search, browse and buy at www.iwm.org.uk/collections. In
addition to Collections Online, you can visit the Visitor Rooms
where you can explore over 8 million photographs, thousands of
hours of moving images, the largest sound archive of its kind in
the world, thousands of diaries and letters written by people in
wartime, and a huge reference library. To make an appointment,
call (020) 7416 5320, or e-mail mail@iwm.org.uk
Imperial War Museums www.iwm.org.uk

Artist's note

Readers may care to note that the original paintings from which
the battlescenes in this book were prepared are available for
private sale. All reproduction copyright whatsoever is retained by
the publishers. All enquiries should be addressed to:

scorpiopaintings@btinternet.com

The publishers regret that they can enter into no correspondence
upon this matter.

CONTENTS

INTRODUCTION

Designed at the height of World War II, the Projector, Infantry, Anti-Tank, or PIAT, was the quintessentially British answer to a very urgent problem: how to give the humble infantryman the firepower to take on Germany's formidable Panzers. As tank armour thickness increased the .55in projectile from the Boys Anti-Tank Rifle, taken to France in 1939 by the troops of the British Expeditionary Force, could no longer penetrate it – a new weapon was needed.

The PIAT's training manual began by explaining that 'the projector differs radically from other small arms' (Small Arms Training 1943: 1). A distant relative of the World War I German Granatenwerfer 16, a spigot-based grenade-thrower effective out to 330yd, the shoulder-fired PIAT was based on designs by Lieutenant-Colonel L.V.S. (Stewart) Blacker, an inventor and adventurer. The PIAT used the spigot-mortar principle to launch a 2.5lb bomb capable of penetrating armour up to 4in thick.

The early design of the PIAT evolved from Blacker's most famous weapon, the Blacker Bombard, but its development was overseen by Britain's Ministry of Defence 1 (MD1) and Imperial Chemical Industries (ICI), one of the country's key chemical manufacturers. MD1, colloquially known as 'Churchill's Toyshop', became one of the most important weapon development centres of the war, developing weapons for clandestine operatives, Commandos and the regular soldier alike. A team led by Lieutenant-Colonel Millis Jefferis, a career soldier and talented engineer, took the basis of Blacker's design and with considerable assistance from ICI turned it into a functional weapon. Just who should receive the credit for designing the PIAT would later become a point of some contention.

Entering service in 1943, the PIAT scored its first victories during the invasion of Sicily, where it quickly proved itself but also gained a reputation among troops for being heavy, inaccurate and somewhat dangerous to use. While the PIAT had clear limitations the men who used it often overcame them with incredible bravery. No fewer than six Victoria Crosses, Britain's highest decoration for gallantry in the presence of the enemy, were won by men equipped with PIATs, along with dozens of other decorations for actions involving the weapon.

Throughout its service life the PIAT acted as a leveller, giving British and Commonwealth soldiers a fighting chance against enemy tanks, as a desperately needed force multiplier for the Polish Home Army fighting to the last in Warsaw, and as one of a handful of surplus anti-tank weapons used by the Jewish Haganah during the 1948 Arab–Israeli War.

While originally designed as an anti-tank weapon, the PIAT was quickly pressed into service against everything from pillboxes to buildings and even boats. It could be used as a direct-fire weapon, firing straight at its target, or in a secondary role as a light mortar, firing in high arcs at more-distant targets to attack buildings, entrenchments or harass enemy positions.

During the D-Day landings in Normandy the first German armoured vehicle to be knocked out by Allied infantry was destroyed by a PIAT. During airborne operations such as the one to capture the Caen Canal bridge, and later the bridge at Arnhem, the PIAT gave lightly armed paratroopers the edge they needed to face entrenched and heavily armed opponents. In dozens of battles during the campaign to liberate Western Europe and in the war against the Japanese the PIAT proved to be a useful weapon when fighting became heavy and the situation especially serious.

The PIAT's operating system was certainly unconventional. Developing a shoulder-fired weapon capable of firing a heavy shaped-charge bomb required a very strong spring to soak up the recoil created by the movement of the spigot. Even with a powerful spring the recoil was significant. A conventional mortar uses gravity, acting on a bomb dropped into a tube, striking the 'anvil' or striker at the base of the tube, detonating the propellant cartridge and firing the mortar bomb. The spigot mortar, by contrast, is an inversion of the conventional system. Rather than a tube it has a solid rod, the spigot, onto which a projectile is placed, this acting as a guide for the bomb. The propellant cartridge is inside the bomb, rather than at its base, and when the striker is fired – in the PIAT's case the striker projects from the tip of the spigot – the bomb's propellant cartridge is ignited and the bomb is launched from the spigot.

The PIAT had a relatively short service life, largely removed from British service by the late 1940s and officially declared obsolete in 1956. It was ultimately replaced by the more effective rocket-based and recoilless-rifle systems. After the war surplus PIATs soldiered on, seeing action in conflicts around the world from Palestine to Indochina to Indonesia.

Today, the PIAT is often mocked or misunderstood as the odd spring-powered British bazooka. While the PIAT proved to be an evolutionary dead end for portable anti-tank weapons, however, it provided much-needed firepower for soldiers who had previously had little more than rifles and hand grenades with which to face enemy tanks. When it entered service the PIAT was an essential weapon and its adoption and use has to be put into context. Hopefully, this book will go some way to help provide that context and show how important and useful the weapon actually was.

A German Granatenwerfer 16 grenade-thrower, part of the Small Arms School Corps Infantry Weapons Collection Trust. (Author's photograph)

DEVELOPMENT
Springs and shaped charges

ORIGINS

For a relatively simple weapon the development of the PIAT was anything but. Before we discuss the development of the PIAT itself, however, it is important to examine the development of Lieutenant-Colonel Stewart Blacker's earlier designs including the equally fascinating Blacker Bombard. His work developing spigot-based weapons began in the early 1930s.

Blacker had developed a series of bomb-launching weapons, with patents granted for both standalone weapons and systems which attached to a soldier's rifle. His keen sense of history and penchant for antiquarian nomenclature can be seen in the names for some of his weapons. He named his first spigot mortar after the 'Arbalest', a type of medieval crossbow with a metal limb; and he famously dubbed his later anti-tank weapon the 'Bombard', after a kind of large medieval muzzle-loading cannon.

In the late 1930s Blacker submitted the Arbalest, or more officially, the 'No. 8 Infantry Bomb Thrower', a light spigot mortar, for trials. Blacker's July 1940 patent for the weapon described how a bomb with an internal propellant cartridge was loaded onto a fixed spigot, which could be mounted to a hydraulic buffer to mitigate the mortar's recoil (UK Patent GB572699, 27/07/40). The Arbalest was rejected, after a series of trials, in May 1939, with the Ordnance Board ruling that Blacker's weapon was over-complicated compared to conventional mortars (Ordnance Board Proceeding 1605, 02/06/39). It was rejected in favour of a 50mm conventional mortar originally designed by a Spanish company, Esperanza y Cia, which became the 2in mortar used by British and Commonwealth forces throughout World War II. During the same year the British Army also adopted a new infantry-section anti-tank weapon, the Boys Anti-Tank Rifle.

When World War II began the British infantryman could call upon two weapons to deal with enemy armoured vehicles. The first was the 2-pdr anti-tank gun; the second weapon, which was the infantry platoon's more immediate asset, was the Boys Anti-Tank Rifle. Developed at the Royal Small Arms Factory at Enfield by a design team led by Captain Henry C. Boys, the Assistant Superintendent of Design, the .55in bolt-action rifle initially fired a 930-grain bullet at 2,450ft/sec. The rifle weighed a formidable 36lb unloaded, with a loaded five-round magazine adding another 2lb 7oz. According to a 1942 Canadian Army manual, the rifle was in principle capable of penetrating armour 0.91in thick at 100yd, but if the armour was sloped this capability decreased significantly (Canadian Army Boys Anti-Tank Rifle Manual, 1942).

The Boys was woefully inadequate for combating Germany's formidable PzKpfw III medium tank, which had frontal armour 1.18in thick. The rifle's shortcomings were recognized even before fighting in the Low Countries and France in 1940 began, with the 1937 manual for the rifle stating that the Boys was 'essentially a weapon of surprise' and suitable only for engaging 'light-armoured fighting vehicles' (Small Arms Training 1939: 5). The 1942 Canadian Army manual recommended that when engaging a PzKpfw III 'fire should be aimed, if it is possible, at vulnerable points' such as the gun mantle and turret joint 'to cause burring over of working surfaces and thus produce jamming' (Canadian Boys Manual 1942: 4). This was a truly desperate course of action. The recoil

This incomplete spigot weapon, part of the Ridgeway Military and Aviation Research Group's Historical Collection, is believed to be one of Blacker's early spigot-mortar prototypes. It would have had a base plate and a bipod like a conventional mortar. (Author's photograph)

of the Boys was also punishing and it was best fired from a standing position, resting on a solid surface.

Following Operation *Crusader*, the British winter 1941 offensive to relieve besieged Tobruk, the Eighth Army's staff looked to learn lessons from the fighting. They could find no instances of the Boys Anti-Tank Rifle actually being used effectively against Axis armoured vehicles (TNA WO 106/2255), all of which served to further underline the weapon's obsolescence.

The disastrous Battle of France and the evacuation from Dunkirk in May–June 1940 placed the British Army in a precarious position. The Army desperately sought an answer to its lack of infantry anti-tank weapons, ramping up production of the 2-pdr anti-tank gun and also seeking new, cheaper weapons to fill the gap. In response, the Blacker Bombard was part of a larger group of less conventional weapons which were hastily developed in the early 1940s.

BLACKER'S BOMBARD

The Bombard was the first weapon Blacker developed with the assistance of Military Intelligence Research. MI(R)c had been formed in the months preceding the outbreak of war and was initially run out of a small office at the War Office, but within months this organization had taken over some offices at the International Broadcasting Company's premises at 35 Portland Place, London. MI(R)c was responsible for the development of the Limpet magnetic anti-ship mine, the 'Sticky Bomb', the 'Time Pencil' fuze and a host of other bombs, mines and gadgets.

With the formation of the Special Operations Executive (SOE) on 22 July 1940, Winston Churchill, acting as both Prime Minister and Minister of Defence, decided to take MI(R)c under his direct control; as such the department became Ministry of Defence 1 (MD1), jokingly referred to by some as 'Churchill's Toyshop'. MD1 continued to grow and later, when its Portland Place premises suffered bomb damage, the organization moved to a country house, *The Firs*, in Whitchurch, Buckinghamshire. There, the spacious house and grounds allowed MD1 to expand and begin production and testing of weapons and devices on site. The establishment would eventually grow to have 250 staff.

In its final form the Blacker Bombard, or 29mm Spigot Mortar as it was officially known, could fire either a 20lb anti-tank projectile filled with 8.75lb of Nobel 808 high explosive, which compressed against armour and detonated, or a 14lb anti-personnel round which used the standard 3in mortar bomb warhead, filled with 1.7lb of high explosive and mounted to a specially designed tail unit. The anti-tank projectile was launched by a 270-grain cordite charge, located at the top of the tail tube. It had an effective range of up to 150yd but it was most effective between 75yd and 100yd. The anti-personnel round had a rated maximum range of 785yd with an effective blast radius of 100yd. The Bombard itself was not considered man-portable for substantial distances, with the action

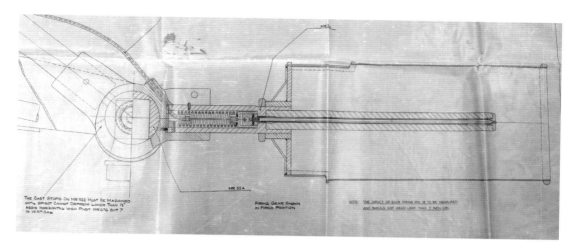

The CAST STOPS ON MR 922 MUST BE MACHINED
UNTIL SPIGOT CANNOT DEPRESS LOWER THAN 15°
ABOVE HORIZONTAL WHEN PIVOT MR 976 SHT 7
IS VERTICAL

FIRING GEAR SHOWN
IN FIRED POSITION

NOTE: THE SPACE OF EACH FIRING PIN IS TO BE MEASURED
AND SHOULD NOT LEAD LESS THAN 2 INCH LBS

MR 33 A

A detail from the Bombard design drawing, drawn in 1941 by ICI showing the spigot. (Teesside Archives)

weighing 112lb while the mount and four legs weighed a further 232lb, giving a total weight of 344lb.

In his memoir, Blacker recalled testing the new weapon against an abandoned Matilda II infantry tank at Pirbright Ranges on Chobham Ridges in Surrey. He stated that six or so impacts perforated the tank's 3in armour with large holes, knocking the vehicle into small pieces and blowing the turret off (Blacker 2006). The Ordnance Board, however, showed little interest in this unconventional weapon designed by an eccentric inventor and built by a department which actively undermined the Board.

With a working prototype of the Bombard in hand, a demonstration was arranged for Churchill at Chequers, the official country residence of the prime minister, on 18 August 1940. Stuart MacRae, MD1's second-in-command, recorded in his diary that a 23lb bomb was demonstrated; the prime minister was impressed and gave the project the green light, authorizing £5,000 for the purpose (MacRae 2012: 95). On 20 September, Blacker reported that testing against a cruiser tank, reinforced with additional 1.25in-thick armour plate, at a range of 75yd resulted in the front plate of the turret being 'punched through with a large hole'; after inspecting the tank's interior, Blacker concluded that its crew would 'have been macerated' (Blacker to Wyndham, 20/09/40). On the strength of this report Professor Frederick A. Lindemann, later Lord Cherwell, in his capacity as chief scientific adviser to the British government, wrote to Churchill suggesting that the Bombard be considered for immediate production, noting the weapon's ease of manufacture and relative cheapness (Lindemann to Churchill, 24/09/40).

In December 1940, Blacker optimistically recommended equipping infantry battalions with no fewer than 24 Bombards each to replace all of the battalion's Boys Anti-Tank Rifles, 3in mortars and anti-tank guns, and also suggested mounting the Bombard on motorcycles. Refinement of the Bombard design continued into the spring of 1941, and following a successful demonstration at Bisley Camp in Surrey in April, GHQ Home Forces noted that the Bombard's performance during the demonstration

Members of the Shropshire Home Guard practise operating a Blacker Bombard mounted on a sunken pedestal mount, built in the centre of a circular trench. This allowed a 360-degree arc of fire and afforded some protection to the Bombard crews, especially the loader. Over 300 of these Bombard positions were built across Britain, along the coast, at strategic chokepoints and in defence of airfields. They were to be manned by local Home Guard and regular Army units to slow down any German advance and give the main field force time to concentrate and counter-attack. (© IWM H 30181)

'fully justified its adoption as an anti-tank weapon both by regular formations and the Home Guard' (TNA WO 199/191-1913). An initial order for 14,000 29mm Spigot Mortars and 3.5 million rounds of ammunition was placed.

ICI, the firm responsible for manufacturing the Nobel 808 explosive used in the Bombard's bombs, were given the contract to produce not only the ammunition but also the new weapons themselves. ICI even set up a Special Arms Department at Witton, near Birmingham, to lead production of the project. The engineering drawings arrived at ICI's Billingham plant in County Durham on 21 June 1941 and production began that July, with ICI acting as the lead contractor and about 150 subcontractors providing various Bombard components. At its peak, ICI Billingham was able to produce 776 Bombards per week. ICI completed its Bombard manufacturing contacts by May 1942, with 19,000 weapons produced at a cost of just over £33,000, roughly equivalent to £1.4m at the time of writing. Between 1941 and 1942, ICI also produced 2.66 million Bombard bombs (ICI/HR/1/14938: 32).

The new anti-tank weapons began reaching Home Guard units in October 1941, with a Home Guard training school, established in Buxton in Derbyshire, running eight courses between November and December. Despite some dissenting opinions, the Bombard was the most formidable weapon available to the Home Guard in 1941–43, its firepower and relative effectiveness far surpassing anything else in the Home Guard's arsenal. By May 1942, 22,149 Bombards had been issued to units stationed in Britain, while 2,815 had been shipped to units abroad ('Bombards and Their Ammunition, Situation' 28/05/42). Over 18,000 Bombards would enter Home Guard service by 1943, with Ministry of Supply records showing that 32,195 Bombards were manufactured in total (TNA AVIA 22/576, MOS).

ENTER THE PIAT

The Blacker Bombard's excessive weight effectively precluded it from being used as an offensive weapon. Britain's soldiers needed something lighter which could be quickly brought into action. As early as September 1940, Blacker had described a 'hand bombard': a weapon with comparable armour-piercing power to that of an anti-tank rifle, greater firepower than a Bren light machine gun, better accuracy than a mortar, weight and handiness similar to that of a rifle as well as 'extreme simplicity, low cost, and suitability for mass production' ('Air Infantry 1941', Blacker, 30/09/40). In January 1941, Blacker confirmed to Professor Lindemann that he was continuing development of the 'hand bombard' and a month later pushed for it to be considered for priority development (Blacker to Lindemann 11/01/41). Despite this, it seems that little progress was made by October 1941, when Blacker wrote a memorandum outlining the history of his spigot-based weapons and noted that 'before this weapon [the hand bombard] can be brought to the "production" stage it is necessary to construct some further prototypes for additional testing' ('Development of the Bombard, Baby Bombard and Arbalest', 30/10/41).

Stuart MacRae described the beginnings of what would eventually become the PIAT in his book. Jefferis reportedly found a rudimentary prototype of a 'shoulder gun' built by Blacker in MD1's workshop. Jefferis telephoned Blacker to ask if he minded him trying to develop his idea. MacRae described the prototype as a long, rusty spring with a few components attached (MacRae 2012: 195). Jefferis' first prototype used the standard 2in mortar round outfitted with a special tail tube and fins. Testing proved the concept, but the recoil proved to be unpleasant. Calculations on spring compression led to the building of a second prototype. With the basic design proven to be workable, the effectiveness of the 2in mortar round as a 'tank-buster' came into question. In response, Jefferis began developing an innovative shaped-charge bomb.

At the same time Blacker also continued development of his own design. By February 1942, prototypes from both designers were ready to be tested at Bisley Camp. The first test took place on 11 February, and on the 14th a meeting with the Ministry of Supply and Major-General E.M.C. Clarke, the Director of Artillery, was held to decide how best to proceed. The report from the meeting represents the best description of the prototypes, describing them as 'the same in principle, the differences being subsidiary mechanical ones' ('Notes of Meeting in Room 270 Ministry of Supply, Subject: Shoulder Bombard' 14/12/42). Blacker's projector was the lighter of the two, weighing 21.5lb and described as having 'a single moving part, i.e. spigot and 'mass' being integral, side loading, as in the Martini-Henry rifle, and capable of being cocked in the lying position' (ibid.). The weapon is described as firing a 3in projectile, weighing 2lb 6oz, at a muzzle velocity of 225ft/sec with a charge of 28 grains of cordite. Jefferis' projector was slightly heavier than its rival, weighing 28lb; it was characterized by having 'a separate false nose to the spigot, the bomb

This photograph of Jefferis' projector prototype, taken some time in 1942, shows a much shorter weapon with a pair of grips and no bomb-support tray. The weapon was cocked via a cocking line and stirrup which projected out of the right side of the projector. (Nuffield College, Cherwell Papers, G272/22 35.1)

being loaded backwards from the muzzle on to it, whilst the cocking was by a wire cable to a lug working down a slot cut in the wall of the main casing tube' (ibid.). Jefferis' projector fired a slightly larger 3.5in bomb, which weighed 2lb 13oz, at a muzzle velocity of 270ft/sec. The bomb was launched by a charge of 52 grains of cordite.

ICI's representative at the meeting, F.E. Smith, asked the Director of Artillery if ICI was to be responsible for development and production. Having been involved in the project since January 1942, the firm was the obvious choice to take on the work. The Director of Artillery agreed and ICI was directed to take over the development of the weapons, with prototypes of both to be built with some minor changes. Blacker's projector had to be scaled up slightly to fire Jefferis' 3.5in bomb, while Jefferis' projector needed to be redesigned to remove the slot down the side of the weapon and allow it to be cocked from a prone position.

It was decided that 'three or more pilot models for production were to be made … incorporating the best features of each gun' ('Notes of Meeting in Room 270…'14/12/42). ICI's own history of its war work explained that 'while the principle of the shoulder gun had been worked out by MD1 and models had been made to demonstrate its action, every part of the gun and ammunition required careful consideration and experiment in order to perfect a design which would meet service requirements' (ICI/HR/1/14938: 341). The Director of Artillery was anxious that production of the new weapons should begin no later than August, giving ICI and MD1 eight months to develop an anti-tank projector suitable for mass production.

The Director of Artillery and the Ministry of Supply stipulated that the weapon should weigh no more than 28lb – significantly lighter than the Boys Anti-Tank Rifle – and should use the Mk II Bren bipod and 'if possible a type of sight already in production' ('Notes of Meeting in Room 270 …' 14/12/42). It was decided that a 'shute or trough' should be used to enable rapid loading. One of the most interesting suggestions was that a fully retracted spigot was not desirable to enable the bomb to be loaded onto something; this suggestion was later abandoned and the PIAT's spigot retracted back into the casing fully. It was also stipulated that the next model should

A soldier demonstrates how the loaded Jefferis projector is aimed. Note the three bomb-carrying holsters he wears, with pointed noses to support the bomb. (Nuffield College, Cherwell Papers, G272/22 35.1)

THE MEN BEHIND THE PIAT

Stewart Blacker

Latham Valentine Stewart Blacker (1 October 1887–19 April 1964) was a British Army officer, inventor and adventurer. He joined the Indian Army in 1907, learnt to fly in 1911 and during World War I joined the Royal Flying Corps as an artillery observer. After the war he took part in expeditions in Persia. Throughout the 1920s, he was attached to the Imperial General Staff, working in the Military Intelligence section dealing with Russia and Eastern Europe. At the same time he began developing his own weapon designs. He was granted his first patent in 1924, for an innovative mortar with a recoil mitigation system. Throughout the 1920s and 1930s he patented a series of designs which focused on launching grenades and other projectiles of various sizes.

In 1932, Blacker retired from the Indian Army and was subsequently commissioned into the Territorial Army's 58 Field Regiment, Royal Artillery, being appointed its commanding officer in 1934. In 1933, he joined the Houston–Mount Everest Expedition as chief observer, becoming part of the first expedition successfully to fly over Mount Everest, photographing the summit.

Blacker was 52 at the outbreak of World War II and unable to accompany his regiment to France. At the time of the evacuation from Dunkirk in May–June 1940, he was without assignment. By the summer of 1940, he found himself loosely attached to MI(R)c, which was tasked with developing weapons for irregular warfare. Here, he found support for his anti-tank spigot mortar which became the Blacker Bombard. Blacker continued to develop his spigot-based designs after the war, patenting improvements as late at 1958. He died in 1964, aged 76.

Millis Jefferis

Millis Rowland Jefferis (9 January 1899–5 September 1963) was educated at the Royal Military Academy, Woolwich, Surrey, which specialized in training artillery and engineer officers. He was commissioned into the Royal Engineers in the summer of 1918, and continued his training at the School of Military Engineering at Chatham in Kent, later joining the British occupying army in the Rhineland. He spent time in India in the 1920s and was awarded the Military Cross in 1923 for gallantry during operations in Waziristan. He was promoted captain in 1929, served in India throughout the 1930s and was promoted major in 1938. With the outbreak of war looking increasingly likely, Jefferis was recalled to Britain and assigned to head up MI(R)c, which was tasked with developing specialized equipment and weapons for clandestine and raiding purposes. In the spring of 1939, he wrote a pamphlet, 'How to Use High Explosives', which became the cornerstone of SOE and Commando training.

In April 1940, Jefferis joined the Allied expedition to Norway, ostensibly to assist in the demolition of key railway infrastructure, but arrived too late to take part in the campaign. During the retreat he damaged two bridges before being evacuated back to Britain. On his return he wrote a detailed report on the situation in Norway and was Mentioned in Despatches for his actions.

Throughout the war he oversaw and led the development of a plethora of weapons and gadgets, including the 'Sticky Bomb', various fuzes and detonators, the 'Beehive' charge and the naval mines used in Operation *Royal Marine*. Stuart MacRae, Jefferis' second-in-command and close friend, described him vividly, contrasting his pugnacious appearance with the agility of his mind (MacRae 2012: 16). MacRae recognized his friend as an idiosyncratic character and also described him as irritable, introverted and somewhat moody on occasion. Even Blacker, who allegedly irritated Jefferis, admired him, describing Jefferis' mind as being full of ingenious schemes. Similarly, Churchill referred approvingly to Jefferis' fertile intellect (Blacker 2006).

Jefferis was promoted lieutenant-colonel in April 1941, brigadier in May 1942, and finally major-general in May 1945, and was knighted the same year (*The London Gazette*, 14/08/45). After the war he became the Engineer-in-Chief in India and later Pakistan before returning to Britain in 1950, retiring three years later (*The London Gazette*, 14/08/53). He died in 1963, aged 64.

be cocked by a 'moveable shoulder piece connected with a rod down the centre of the weapon' ('Minute of the Meeting held at the Adelphi on Saturday 14 February 1942, To Discuss the Production of an Infantry Anti-Tank Weapon on the Lines of the Models Put Forward by Lt. Colonel Jefferis and Lt. Colonel Blacker').

Within three days the two competing prototypes had arrived at ICI Billingham and development work began in earnest. ICI's account of the development suggests that the Director of Artillery had initially favoured Jefferis' design, and that 'by way of precaution, they [the engineers at Billingham] decided to prepare two new designs, one based on the Jefferis model favoured by the Director of Artillery and the other on the Blacker model' (ICI/HR/1/14938: 342). Within a week the engineers at ICI Billingham had new prototypes ready to test, with the weapon based on Jefferis' design designated the Type A, while Blacker's design was designated the Type B. Both were designed to fire the bomb developed by Jefferis. Four Type A projectors and one Type B were built, and the first firing tests were carried out on 17 February. Following disappointing tests with the Type A projector, however, the focus was shifted to the Type B with its combined sleeve bolt and spigot.

The first test of the Type B took place on 28 February, with ten rounds fired with no failures; according to ICI this led the focus of development to be shifted to the Blacker-based Type B (ICI/HR/1/14938: 342). The Type B had a number of desirable features, including Blacker's fixed spigot, trigger mechanism and bomb-support tray, while the cocking mechanism was developed by ICI and MD1. These early prototypes allowed a process of trial and error to the point where calculations could be used to work out the necessary spring strength and the spigot and sleeve mass required.

By early April a further developed projector, the Type C, had been developed and tested; at 34lb it proved too heavy, however, exceeding the War Office's 28lb requirement. A compromise model with features from the Type B and Type C was assembled; designated the Type D, it was tested at Bisley Camp in late April. Further refinement continued and a final trial at Bisley Camp was held on 8 July.

Just as the final trials were taking place ICI Billingham endured two nights of Luftwaffe bombing, on 7/8 and 8/9 July 1942. Both high-explosive and incendiary bombs fell on the plant, destroying fuel tanks, damaging a number of buildings and destroying some of the PIAT's production gauges. Dozens of fires were started by the incendiary bombs and the nearby village was also hit. ICI Billingham was bombed for a third time in late July. These attacks slowed initial production of the PIAT, but the first batch of 35 weapons left the plant on 26 August, meeting the deadline set by the Director of Artillery back in February (ICI/HR/1/14938: 347).

ICI's internal designation for the final model of projector was the Type MG, with all of the production drawings for the PIAT marked 'MG' from May 1942 onwards. The design was finalized by the Chief Superintendent of Armament Design, Captain C.T. Nuthall, on 19 May 1942; its official War Office design designation was D.D(E)3247, but its in-service designation would be Projector, Infantry, Anti-Tank Mk I.

In April 1942, ICI had informed the Ministry of Supply that the cost of starting up mass-production of the PIAT and its ammunition would total £82,445, the equivalent of £3.8m today. This sum would pay for plant, machine tools and gauges, installation costs and building alterations (MoS to Treasury Office, 17/04/42). Production in the United States was initially considered, but in the event, manufacture was entirely undertaken

OPPOSITE
ICI's final design drawing for the PIAT, November 1943, showing the adjustable monopod, straight butt and quadrant sight.
(Teesside Archives)

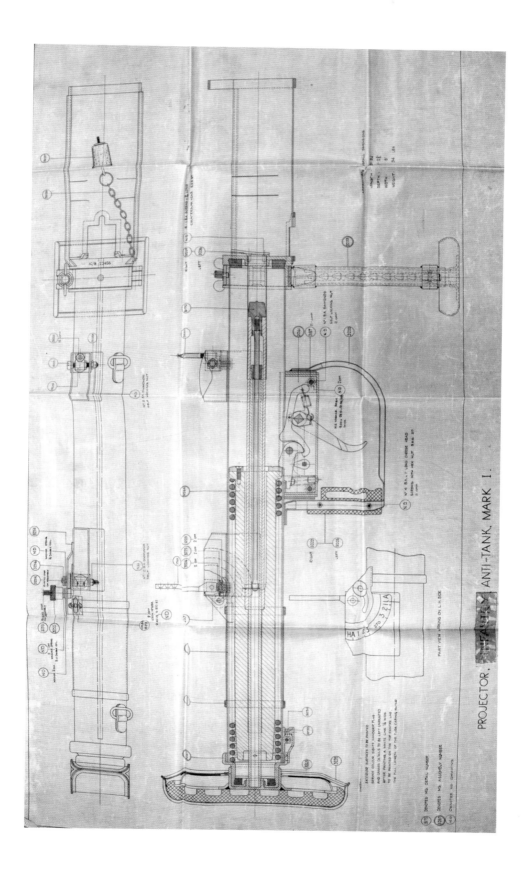

PROJECTOR. INFANTRY ANTI-TANK. MARK I.

Projector, Infantry, Anti-Tank Mk I

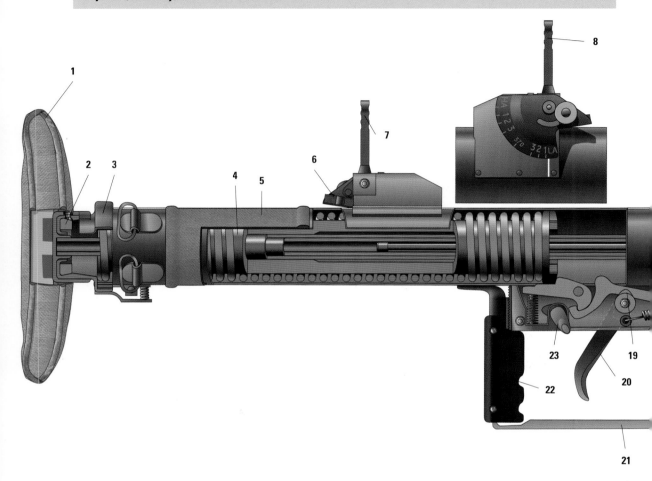

1. Butt
2. Rear buffer
3. Rear end cap
4. Sleeve bolt
5. Gaiter
6. Spirit level
7. Rear sight
8. Rear sight (left-side view)
9. Front sight
10. Loading clip
11. Left projectile guide plate
12. Tail unit
13. Body rear
14. Union ring
15. Fore body
16. Tail tube

17. Spigot guide rod tube cork stopper
18. Adjustable monopod
19. Tripping-lever link
20. Trigger
21. Trigger guard
22. Grip
23. Safety-catch lever
24. Mainspring
25. Cocking rod
26. Aiming line
27. Spigot guide tube
28. Firing pin
29. Tripping lever
30. Tripping-lever spring
31. Sear spring
32. Sear

33. Removable dust excluder
34. Tail fin
35. Cartridge
36. C.E. pellet
37. Wood spacer
38. Steel cone
39. Felt washer
40. Spring
41. Fuze-hole plug
42. Fuze holder
43. Detonator No. 66 Mk I
44. Cordtex
45. Explosive 808
46. Cup
47. Felt plug and disc

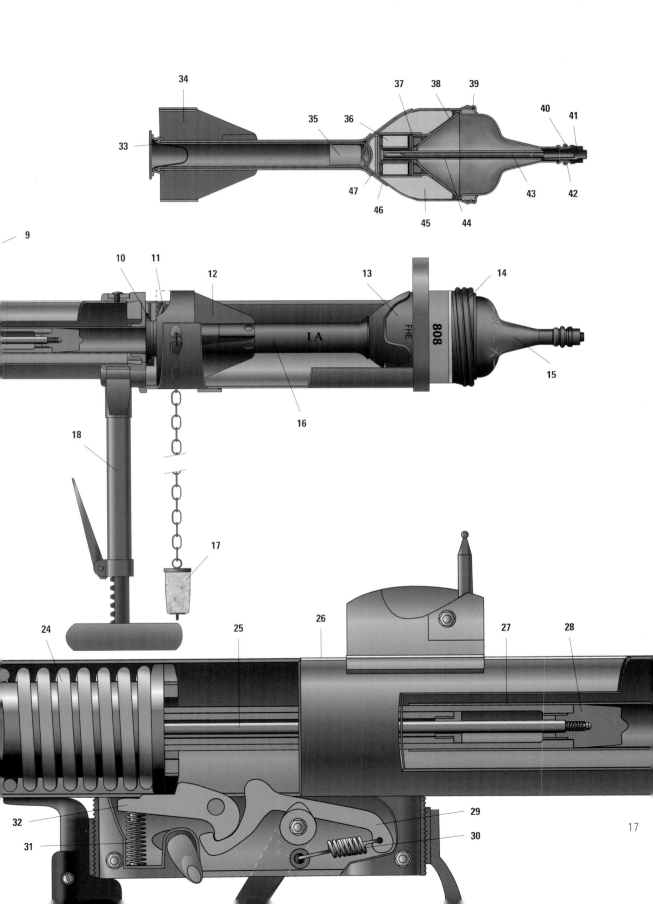

34

37 38 39

40 41

33 35 36

47

46 45 44 43 42

9

10 11 12 13 14

18 16 15

17

24 25 26 27 28

32

31 29

30

17

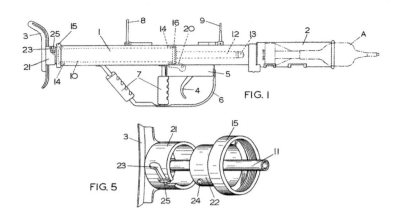

A patent protecting the PIAT's basic design was filed in Jefferis' name in August 1942. (UK Patent Office, GB579158)

by factories in Britain. Overseen by ICI, seven companies were initially contracted to produce PIATs. In total, the Treasury expected the production of 100,000 PIATs and 1 million rounds of ammunition to cost £200,000 (£9.2m today).

Getting the PIAT into production required many changes to the design and saw the weapon eventually gain nearly 10lb in weight. Much of the PIAT's weight lay in its substantial 4lb spring and its 12lb spigot and sleeve bolt. Its sights, monopod, trigger assembly and butt weighed 6lb while the body casing and endplates weighed 10lb (OB Proc. No. AG1109, 05/05/43). In all, the PIAT was 39in long and weighed 34.5lb.

The first 1,000 production PIAT Mk Is were delivered in November 1942. Just three months later, the Army was optimistic about the PIAT's potential versatility, hoping to use it as a mortar and develop smoke and high-explosive rounds and extend the weapon's range to 500yd (OB Proc. No. AG1,000, 15/01/43).

When the PIAT entered production it had a set of flip-up sights; its rear sight had two apertures, for 70yd and 100yd. The pistol grip was made of two plastic panels and a canvas gaiter provided a cheek rest. The weapon had a non-adjustable A-frame front support and a curved butt, covered by a canvas pad. The body of the PIAT was not Parkerized like other weapons but granodized, a phosphate coating which was rust-resistant. The weapons were painted with a coat of red-oxide primer and two coats of brown paint. A long white line to aid indirect firing was then added along the length of the top of the body casing. The serial number was stamped into the top of the weapon's body casing at the front.

The PIAT's dynamic spigot weighed about 12lb; once the weapon was fired this moved rearward at a speed of 25ft/sec, producing 41 newtons of recoil force which was directed back into the operator's shoulder. The recoil impulse was said to feel less like a kick and more like a steady thrust. Once compressed the spring had a formidable pressure of 200lb per inch of compression that launched the bomb at a velocity of 265ft/sec (*The Infantry Projector*, 16/05/42).

THE PIAT'S AMMUNITION

The bombs fired by the PIAT required just as much experimentation and development as the weapon itself. It was no easy task to design a bomb which was powerful enough to knock out Germany's most formidable tanks, and which exploded as it impacted the target but was also safe to transport and manoeuvre in action.

The ammunition was developed by engineers from MD1 and ICI. While conventional explosive projectiles were initially developed, the focus quickly shifted to the use of a shaped charge rather than a poultice charge – one which flattened against the target before detonating, like that used by the Bombard. There were some initial issues getting the heavy projectiles to fly stably, but according to MacRae these were eventually resolved with the addition of a drum tail with fins (MacRae 2012: 196).

The PIAT used a HEAT (High Explosive Anti-Tank) projectile. On detonation this shaped charge created an intense localized heat which punched a hole through a tank's armour and created carnage inside. The colossal pressure generated liquefied fragments of armour plate and the intense heat penetrated the interior of the vehicle, causing considerable damage, detonating any stored ammunition and killing or maiming members of the crew.

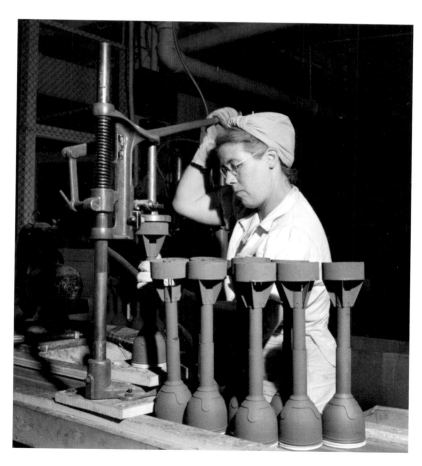

A female worker assembles PIAT bomb tail units in Orillia, Ontario, Canada, June 1944. (Library and Archives Canada, MIKAN No. 3197637)

The Mk IA (above) and Mk II (below) projectiles.

The outer shell of the bomb was made from simple stamped sheet-metal. It was filled with Nobel 808 explosive, and later a 50:50 mix of RDX and TNT, packed behind a steel cone. A small brass propellant cartridge at the base of the bomb, when ignited by the spigot's firing pin, provided enough energy to launch the round with a muzzle velocity of about 265ft/sec. To detonate the charge without making the bomb casing longer or heavier by positioning the explosive further back, a forward fuze was devised with a narrow tube, containing a length of Cordtex instantaneous detonating cord, running from the contact fuze to the explosive at the back of the bomb. The bombs were shipped with their propellant cartridges fitted but their fuzes separate, attached to the tail of the bomb, held in a fuze carrier. This unusual design feature enabled the explosive to detonate just before direct contact with the target's armour. By exploding just ahead of the target the focus of the blast was intensified, maximizing the shaped charge's penetrative capabilities.

As the PIAT began to be issued, a number of problems with its ammunition were identified, with rounds glancing off targets or failing to detonate after striking. The issue was found to be caused by the No. 425 contact fuze, which needed a strong striker spring to prevent handling accidents. The need for a graze fuze was recognized as early as December 1942, primarily for the bombs to be effective in both the anti-tank and anti-personnel roles (OB Proc. No. AG 1,000, 15/01/43). As a result, the self-arming No. 426 fuze, which armed during flight, was eventually developed, ensuring that the fuze was safe to handle but more likely to detonate downrange. An ICI investigation into a 'considerable number of rejections' due to insufficient penetration was found to be the result of 'empty defects' and issues with voids forming during the bomb-filling process (SUPP 22/26). As a result a number of filling methods were experimented with; finally, a method devised by the Chief Superintendent Armament Research was adopted.

Efforts were also made to improve the ammunition's performance, safety and ease of manufacture. The Mk I projectile weighed 3lb and was filled with 1lb of Nobel 808 explosive; the improved Mk IA had a reinforced flange. The Mk II was modified to simplify production, with a narrower – 3.25in rather than 3.5in – liner cone and a slightly lighter overall weight of 2.5lb. The Mk III incorporated the improved No. 426 graze fuze, while the final Mk 4 variant was modified in an attempt to prevent the flying of fragments back towards the operators (RARDE Branch Memorandum 31/78 (MA2)). The improved No. 426 graze fuze was more sensitive, with a ball tip which increased detonation rates and reduced the likelihood of the round glancing off without exploding.

Another of the major issues with the PIAT was the wounding of the operator by fragments seemingly ricocheting back from the target. One of the first instances of this occurred during an early demonstration at Bisley Camp when a member of the Small Arms School Corps (SASC) was badly wounded by a piece of metal which passed through the slot in the screen and hit him (MacRae 2012: 196). A similar, if not the same, incident was described by the SASC's Quartermaster Sergeant Instructor Harry Driffield, who along with another member of the SASC, Archie Fordham, was demonstrating the PIAT from a carefully prepared bunker with the weapon firing through a small aperture. When the PIAT was fired, the projectile exploded on the target, a steel plate, at a range of less than 100yd. A fragment of metal was thrown back towards the two men and hit Fordham in the shoulder (Driffield 2002: 36). Fordham was badly wounded, with the fragments deflecting into his lung.

In May 1942, the problem was identified as partially being caused by parts of 'a brass ring (part of the propellant charge cylinder) flying to the rear with considerable velocity. This was considered very dangerous and appropriate alterations are being made to this particular part' (*The Infantry Projector*, 16/5/42). Further investigation revealed that fragments were being projected down the bomb's tail tube back towards the operator at speeds of up to 3,000ft/sec (RARDE Branch Memorandum 31/78 (MA2). In June 1944, another incident occurred during a PIAT training session held by the 25th New Zealand Infantry Battalion, when fragments flew back from the target and slightly wounded two men. This issue was addressed by the Mk 4 bomb, introduced a month later, which had steel discs to prevent fragments travelling down the tube.

One of the simplest improvements to the PIAT was made to the spring steel loading clips attached to the base of the bombs. These helped to hold the projectile in the weapon while the operator moved with a loaded PIAT or aimed it downwards, keeping the bomb aligned with the spigot. Testing conducted during the summer of 1943 showed that use of an improved four-prong loading clip reduced failures of the weapon to re-cock. The move to the new four-prong clip was approved in August 1943.

A number of attempts to develop different projectiles for the PIAT were made during its service. In July 1942, attempts were made to use the PIAT's bomb to deliver a chemical weapon. The concept was to use the PIAT's hollow-charge warhead to punch through the armour of a tank and then distribute a chemical-warfare agent inside. The test took place at Britain's Chemical Defence Experimental Station at Porton Down in Wiltshire. A standard projectile was slightly modified by adding a brass cylinder, which was filled with inert magnesium oxide to represent a chemical agent – which in theory would kill the vehicle's crew. When the modified projectile was fired at a tank, it penetrated the armour but no sign of the magnesium oxide was found to have passed into the vehicle. It was concluded that adapting the bomb to carry a chemical agent was not feasible (OB Proc. 960, 3/2/43). Later, a bomb filled with white phosphorus was developed and experimented with, but did not enter service (AORG Report No. 167, 1945). Similarly, efforts were made in 1943 to develop a dedicated high-explosive round for the PIAT, but this was abandoned in early 1944 (OB Proc. AG 1,311, 21/1/44). By the end of the war, approximately 18 million rounds of the PIAT's HEAT ammunition had been manufactured at factories around the world, at a cost of nearly £10m (Royal Commission on Awards to Inventors, 19/11/47).

The Mk III (above) and Mk 4 (below) projectiles.

CHANGES IN SERVICE

Even as the PIAT went into production its limitations were understood, and it was also recognized that a weapon with 'longer range and higher velocity' would be needed (*The Infantry Projector*, 16/5/42). Attempts to improve the PIAT's accuracy, increase its range and lower its weight continued after it entered service. A three-aperture rear sight for ranges of 50yd, 80yd and 100yd replaced the original two-aperture sight; in turn this was subsequently altered to have a 110yd maximum range aperture.

The PIAT went through more than 70 design changes between August 1942 and April 1943, the majority of which were spurred by the desire to develop the weapon's secondary role as a light mortar. The first effort to assist in indirect fire was the painting of a white line along the top of the body casing in May 1942.

The PIAT was initially tested as a light mortar with an additional bipod and mortar quadrant sight; however, in October 1942, SASC trials found that the PIAT performed well enough with an extendable monopod developed by ICI. Tests found the PIAT to be more accurate and produce less smoke on firing than the 2in mortar, and its bomb was found to have 'considerable possibilities as an anti-personnel bomb' with a 15ft blast radius (OB Proc. AG, 1,000, 15/01/43). In December 1942, an official requirement was issued, but it was recognized that the lifespan of the spring was likely to be too short for additional use as a light mortar.

A number of monopods and bipods were evaluated. A curved stabilizing spade attachment was briefly considered but quickly rejected, and the PIAT's curved butt was straightened to allow it to act as a more stable base. A 2in mortar quadrant sight was tested but a simpler sight graduated out to 370yd was selected in June 1943. With its new expanded role the lifespan of the PIAT's spring became a key concern as troops would be using the weapon much more often. The spring life of early prototype PIATs was estimated to be around 200 rounds, but by September 1942, ICI had improved this to 'the order of 400–500 rounds' (ICI to OB, 16/09/42). A concerted effort was made to improve the spring's lifespan even further. It was initially suggested that each PIAT should have three additional spare springs, but attempts were made to increase the spring's life to a minimum of 1,000 rounds. ICI experimented extensively, and by June 1943 had managed to double the spring's lifespan. This was achieved by 'scragging': compressing the spring after heat treatment to minimize deformation,

Another detail of a PIAT in the hands of the Small Arms School Corps Infantry Weapons Collection Trust. ICI developed an adjustable monopod that allowed the PIAT to be elevated up to 40 degrees, with 11 increments. (Author's photograph)

The PIAT's quadrant sight had a tubular spirit level and was graduated out to 370yd with 100yd increments from 100yd to 300yd. The weapon shown here is held by the Small Arms School Corps Infantry Weapons Collection Trust. (Author's photograph)

23

Men of The Royal Australian Regiment train with early-pattern PIATs in Japan, August 1950. Note the A-frame monopod and curved butt. Both PIATs have their practice-bomb adapters fitted. (AWM HOBJ1085)

before blueing the springs, rather than after (OB Proc. No. AG 1140, 10/06/43).

While a second mark of PIAT was never officially designated, the changes made to the weapon were substantial. In addition to the changes to the spring and butt, the original A-frame support was replaced by an adjustable monopod to enable some gross elevation adjustment up to 40 degrees; this became the monopod most commonly associated with the PIAT. The transition took place at the beginning of 1943, with 25,000 PIATs expected to be completed before the changeover. Armourers were directed to update the weapons in theatre, but many photographs show the earlier pattern continuing to be used on the front line into 1945. Many other improvements were considered, including a rotating front support and a tropical shoulder-carrying pad, but none was adopted before the end of World War II.

BLACKER'S LATER DEVELOPMENTS

Blacker continued developing spigot-based designs and improvements for the PIAT once it had entered production, including a number of lightened projectors with narrower body casings and folding bomb-support trays. This lightened projector type was known to the War Office and the Ordnance Board as Design No. 100. While very similar in form and proportions to the production PIAT, Blacker's improved designs differed in almost all of their dimensions and in layout, with the sights in different positions, a folding bomb-support tray, a new design of spigot tube plug and a redesigned butt assembly which included folding footplates and a rubber pad, designed to absorb recoil.

The Design No. 100 projector was first proposed to the Ordnance Board in early 1943, with Blacker describing its features at a meeting on 30 March. Described as 'the new design of PIAT' (OB Proc. No. AG1,083, 30/03/43), Blacker's improved projector fired the same bomb as the PIAT but was significantly lighter, weighing 26lb. Conversely, it was also longer, with surviving prototypes measuring 42in. Blacker compensated for the increase in length by having a bomb-support tray made of spring steel which 'folded back, thus giving a shorter overall length of the projector' (ibid.). The spigot's length of travel was also longer as a result of the longer casing and it had a buffer spring to mitigate felt recoil.

The Design No. 100 projector also had a solid spigot rather than a drilled one, with a separate firing pin. This would have simplified production. The new projector could be disassembled without the need for tools. Unlike the PIAT, the improved projector was said to be easier to cock when lying prone but more difficult when standing. It was also suggested, however, that with the increased length of the weapon, the No. 2 (loader) would be more exposed when loading. The Ordnance Board was curious and ordered two of Blacker's improved projectors for evaluation. Subsequently, in May 1943, the order was increased to six prototypes after Blacker further explained the advantages of the new design (OB Proc. No. AG 1109, 05/05/43).

Examination of surviving prototypes believed to be Design No. 100 projectors found that instead of a canvas gaiter, the improved projectors had a moulded Bakelite cuff, extending from the butt assembly to the rear-sight housing, for the operator to rest his face on. From the surviving, but incomplete, prototypes it is clear that there is a degree of variation between them, with the profile of the folding bomb-support tray differing

This incomplete projector prototype, part of the Ridgeway Military and Aviation Research Group's Historical Collection, is believed to be a Blacker Design No. 100 projector. Sadly, it is missing its monopod and pistol grip. (Author's photograph)

The potential Design No. 100 projector prototype, held by the Ridgeway Military and Aviation Research Group Historical Collection, had a hinged spring steel folding bomb-support tray. Note also the folding front sight and the chain link which hold the spigot tube plug. (Author's photograph)

and some of the dimensions varying slightly, but they appear to have fired the same standard PIAT round.

In December 1943, Blacker's improved projector was scheduled to undergo trials at Bisley Camp and the Proof and Experimental Establishment (P&EE) at Shoeburyness in Essex, with user trials to be conducted by the SASC. The SASC received two Design No. 100 projector prototypes, which were shipped cocked; one of the new weapons was disassembled and reassembled for inspection on arrival. When the first prototype was taken to the range for preliminary test firing, however, it was discovered that the trigger mechanism was non-operable. On inspection it was found that a small screw on the trigger mechanism had sheared off. The second prototype was then removed from its shipping crate and also found to have a sheared screw in its trigger mechanism and could not be fired either. The SASC also reported that the clip retaining the weapon's monopod had broken in transit and described the method of securing the monopod in the firing position as unsatisfactory.

P&EE Shoeburyness had more luck and was able to test Blacker's new lightened PIAT. The object of the trials was to test Blacker's lighter prototype against a standard-issue PIAT. The P&EE reported that ten rounds were fired at 70yd and 100yd and the muzzle velocity of the prototype was found to be comparable to that of the standard PIAT. The accuracy of Blacker's prototype proved to be 'better than with the service

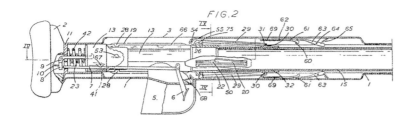

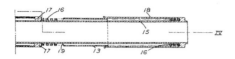

Patent drawing, from May 1944, depicting Blacker's recoil-mitigated projector design. Among the labelled parts are the breech casing (**1**), butt (**2**), pistol grip (**5**), trigger (**6**), tube (**13**), barrel (**15**), sears (**20**), lugs (**26**), arms (**29**), buffer spring (**42**) and pivoted strikers (**63**). (UK Patent Office, GB602304)

projector at 70 yards but about the same at 100 yards' (OB Proc. AG1317, 26/01/44). By the time the reports from the various establishments reached the Ordnance Board, however, it had already been decided (on 4 January 1944) that further development of Blacker's Design No. 100 projector design would be cancelled. The Director of Artillery (Small Arms) ruled that there was 'no requirement for a PIAT Mark II nor for the new Blacker design of PIAT' (ibid.).

Patents for other anti-tank projectors developed by Blacker show that he was experimenting with recoil-mitigation systems. Two patents were filed in June 1943 and May 1944 for a semi-automatic projector; it was not spigot-based and had an almost 'bullpup' layout, with a pair of recuperator springs – recoil springs which return the barrel forward after firing – mounted either side of a telescoping barrel. This very complex and likely weighty design does not appear to have been evaluated by the British Army.

OTHER ALLIED SPIGOT WEAPONS

In the summer of 1945, Major Bernard Schott, the commanding officer of the Aegean section of the Light Raiding Forces, submitted a weapon he called the 'Light Raiding Force PIAT'. The Light Raiding Force PIAT was developed for Commandos who were not able to carry the cumbersome 32lb PIAT. Major Schott's light PIAT weighed just 5.5lb and had a single moving part, dispensing with the spring, body and trigger mechanism of the traditional PIAT. Instead, it consisted of a spigot and an outer firing sleeve with a small stabilizing spade at its base. It used a simple striker with a safety notch, similar to that of the Sten submachine gun.

Without the PIAT's powerful recoil spring the lightened PIAT was more a hand mortar than projector. Its recoil was much more violent, bending its stabilizing spade significantly. In May 1945 Schott's prototype weapon was tested in Italy, by the Weapons Technical Staff of the Mediterranean Area field forces. Their report concluded that the light PIAT was 'not considered a safe weapon to put into the hands of troops'; moreover, 'it is very uncomfortable for the firer, both from blast and shock to the hands and arms, and further at low elevation, extreme care is necessary to avoid minor obstructions in the line of flight' (Light Raiding Force PIAT, Trial Report SA/13/45, MED Area HQ Weapons Technical Staff, 13/06/45).

Schott also submitted what he described as a 'Time Delay PIAT'. The idea was to use a PIAT bomb on a small spigot which could be set up during a raid, at a distance from its target, and left to discharge once the raiding force had withdrawn. Major Schott described the Time Delay PIAT as 'extremely light and cheap' and claimed that a 2ft^2 target could 'easily be hit at 100–120 [yd] with accuracy' (Schott to Weapons Technical Staff Field Forces, May 1945).

Weighing 2.5lb, the Time Delay PIAT consisted of an 18in hollow tube which acted as the spigot onto which the bomb was placed. A ten-minute time-delay pencil fuze was placed in an adaptor and used to detonate the cartridge inside the PIAT bomb's base. Schott also suggested that the

A photograph from the Weapons Technical Staff of the Mediterranean Area field forces' testing of Major Bernard Schott's 'Light Raiding Force PIAT', firing at a low angle. (© Royal Armouries)

A photograph from the testing of Schott's 'Time Delay PIAT' with the spigot supported by a rock at about 20 degrees. The bomb was launched by a time fuze and travelled 80yd. (© Royal Armouries)

Major Cecil Vandepeer Clarke's spigot gun with ball-jointed screw base for securing into a tree. (© IWM MUN 5773)

weapon could be fired by a tripwire. During testing in July 1945, only two of the four test firings were successful and neither bomb managed to reach its target. The test report opined that the idea behind the weapon was sound but it was concluded that it would take considerable training to enable users to set up the weapon to fire accurately. The evaluating officers felt that the Time Delay PIAT was not sufficiently reliable and serviceable to be issued to troops.

With the European conflict over and the war against the Japanese coming to an end, the development of Schott's PIAT adaptations appears to have been abandoned. What Schott did not know, however, was that a very similar weapon had already been developed. Schott's concept is very similar to the spigot gun developed by Major Cecil Vandepeer Clarke. Clarke's spigot gun was a simple system which could be mounted on trees, on a base plate or simply fired from the ground. It could be brought into action rapidly, taking less than 60 seconds to set up and was reportedly able to engage stationary targets up to 200yd away. Unlike the PIAT's shaped-charge HEAT projectile, Clarke's weapon used 3lb of plastic explosive which flattened onto its target before it detonated – much like the Blacker Bombard's bomb. The base had an ingenious ball-joint which enabled the spigot to be aimed once the base was either screwed into a tree or set up on a base plate. A periscope-type sight slid onto the spigot with the approximate range set and the spigot aimed at the target. A

29

SPIGOTS ON LAND AND SEA: THE AVRE AND HEDGEHOG

In addition to the PIAT, other larger, more specialized spigot weapons also saw extensive service during World War II on land and at sea. The 290mm Petard, mounted on the Churchill Armoured Vehicle Royal Engineers (AVRE), could launch 40lb of explosive at targets up to 80yd away. Nicknamed the 'flying dustbin', because of its shape, the round could smash buildings or reinforced pillboxes and destroy roadblocks. Sergeant John Solomon, a driver with 222 Assault Squadron, Royal Engineers, vividly remembered the round's terrific detonation and devastating effect (IWM 11320).

The Anti-Submarine Projector, or 'Hedgehog', was developed by the Directorate of Miscellaneous Weapons Development in conjunction with MD1. It consisted of 24 spigot mortars firing high-explosive projectiles, each weighing 65lb, in a circular or elliptical pattern about 200yd ahead of the sub-hunting vessel. Each Hedgehog bomb was tipped with a contact fuze and the bomb would detonate if it struck a submarine's hull. If the salvo was well aimed the pattern was large enough to ensure at least one or two bombs struck the target. The Hedgehog was deployed aboard Royal Navy and US Navy vessels from 1943 onwards, and is credited with over 40 submarine 'kills'. A number of Landing Craft Assault (LCAs) were fitted with Hedgehogs and dubbed 'Hedgerows'; in theory, these could get close to the beach and help to clear barbed wire or minefields, and a number were used during D-Day, 6 June 1944. On land, the Australian Army briefly experimented with mounting the Hedgehog on a Matilda II infantry tank chassis.

To load the 290mm Petard, the barrel was rotated upward 90 degrees and the loader had to push a bomb up into the weapon while exposed to enemy fire. This photograph shows a Churchill AVRE's Petard with a 'flying dustbin' bomb next to it. (© IWM H 38001)

The Hedgehog anti-submarine spigot-mortar system, fully loaded with 24 high-explosive projectiles, aboard the W-Class destroyer HMS *Westcott*, the first Royal Navy vessel to be fitted with the Hedgehog which replaced the vessel's forward QF 4in Mk V gun. (© IWM A 31000)

tripwire or lanyard was attached to a rod which retained the striker until the spigot was ready to fire; alternatively, a time-delay fuze could also be used.

Clarke's spigot gun was developed in 1943, at SOE's Station XII (Aston House, near Stevenage in Hertfordshire); it was envisaged that it would be used by paratroopers or clandestine agents in occupied territory. The weapon was produced in the US by Division 19 (Miscellaneous Weapons) of the US Office of Scientific Research and Development (OSRD). How much use Clarke's ingenious weapon saw remains unclear; although a detailed training film was produced for the Office of Strategic Services (OSS), a post-war report on the OSRD's work suggested that it did not reach OSS agents in the field. The extent of operational use with SOE is unknown.

USE
The PIAT in action

Before the adoption of the PIAT the British infantryman's principal anti-tank weapons at the outbreak of war were the Boys Anti-Tank Rifle and the No. 68 anti-tank rifle grenade, which, like the Boys, proved to be woefully inadequate. These were later joined by the No. 73 anti-tank grenade, the No. 74 'Sticky Bomb' anti-tank grenade developed by MIR(c) and later the No. 75 Hawkins anti-tank grenade, all of which required even closer proximity to the enemy tank than the PIAT.

Like the PIAT the No. 68 anti-tank rifle grenade used a shaped charge, but its small size meant it could penetrate only 2in of armour. The grenade was fired from a discharger cup which fitted to the muzzle of the rifle. (Lt Tanner/Imperial War Museums via Getty Images)

31

The PIAT began to reach troops just in time for Opearation *Husky*, the Allied invasion of Sicily in July–August 1943, with 19 issued to each infantry battalion: three per rifle company (or one per platoon), with the support company equipped with a further seven PIATs distributed among the carrier and mortar platoons. By late 1943, each brigade support group – a formation intended to provide increased firepower to augment a division's brigades – was equipped with a further seven PIATs. By June 1944, the number of PIATs per infantry battalion had increased to 23; in comparison a US Army infantry battalion fielded a total of 29 M9 'bazooka' anti-tank rocket launchers in 1944. By the end of the war the PIAT had been issued not only to British troops but also to units of every other Commonwealth nation, including Australia, Canada, New Zealand, India and South Africa.

TRAINING WITH THE PIAT

Troops were taught how to use the PIAT over the course of three lessons, each lesson made up of two 40-minute periods, with the instructor's manual calling for plenty of time for practice firing to be scheduled. In reality this was not always possible, and some soldiers recalled firing only a single practice round. All men would receive instruction on the PIAT, in case they were called upon to use one in the field. They were taught how it worked and as how to act as both No. 1 (gunner) and No. 2 (loader). Training was conducted with live PIATs, with drill and inert practice bombs. A dedicated drill-purpose PIAT was never produced despite concerns about wear and tear of working PIATs being used for training purposes. Even as late as 1947, the development of a drill-purpose PIAT was considered, but it was agreed that a significant redesign of the weapon's internal parts would be needed which would compromise its usefulness as a training aid (D. of A. (S.A.) to C.E.A.D, 17/7/47).

During the first lesson the men were introduced to the PIAT. They were taught that although it had an admittedly short effective range, it could take on and knock out enemy armoured vehicles and be used against buildings up to 350yd away. The 1943 manual emphasized the PIAT's 'excellent penetration', informing the class that it could 'penetrate the armour of the latest known types of enemy AFVs and a considerable thickness of reinforced concrete' (Small Arms Training 1943: 2). The first lesson also covered the basic operation of the PIAT and the weapon's maintenance, with the instructor demonstrating cocking and uncocking. The bomb itself was also discussed and the instructor would explain that when ammunition was issued it was loaded with a propellant cartridge but its fuze would not be fitted. Finally, the instructor would explain how to fuze the bomb and how to field-strip the weapon for cleaning.

The second lesson covered the actual use of the PIAT – loading, aiming and firing – with troops practising with drill and inert practice bombs. Troops were taught that when in action or with action imminent, the PIAT should be carried cocked at all times but unloaded until needed, and with the safety catch on and the cork 'muzzle plug' in place. The

THE BLACKER BOMBARD IN SERVICE

Alongside our examination of the use of the PIAT, it is worth briefly examining the deployment of its predecessor, the 29mm Spigot Mortar or Blacker Bombard. Although it is widely believed that the Bombard was almost exclusively issued to Home Guard units, in reality it did see some overseas service. The weapon had been designed to alleviate a shortage of anti-tank weapons and Churchill certainly envisaged its use by both the regular Army and the Home Guard. The Bombard was issued to Home Guard units across Britain but also to regular units defending airfields and manning coastal artillery positions.

Douglas Fitzroy served in his local Home Guard unit while studying at Oxford; he was one of the lucky few who had the opportunity to fire a Bombard at a moving target while training. He recalled that the weapon was close to the ground, making it easy to camouflage, and rated it as a very effective anti-tank weapon for static positions (IWM 20596). The Bombard's unconventional design did not impress all those who saw it. Dave Edwards, a member of the Home Guard in Abergavenny, remembered the strange appearance of the Bombard, with its bicycle-style handles (IWM 32384). Thomas Roome, a young member of the Home Guard in London, recalled the procedure for a Bombard misfire, which entailed pivoting the weapon towards the No. 2 and removing the round (IWM 15485). Sadly, at least one fatal accident occurred during a Bombard demonstration. It was reported in October 1941 that two members of the Home Guard were killed and eight other men were badly wounded in East Sussex when an incorrectly fitted fuze caused a premature detonation.

Ironically, some of the regular troops who encountered the Blacker Bombard were the men of the Royal Artillery's coastal batteries, who were trained to use some of the British Army's largest and most complex artillery. Sergeant Robert Sweeting of 526 Coast Regiment, Royal Artillery, explained that battery personnel were tasked with defending their position; the four Bombards given to his unit were placed along the sea front ahead of the battery (IWM 27089). If attacked overland, the batteries would have to defend themselves and the gunners didn't have a lot of confidence in their primary anti-tank weapon. Lance Bombardier Leonard Stockill, also of 526 Coast Regiment RA, remembered the Bombard as being very basic; he did not rate the weapon highly (IWM 27258).

It wasn't just coastal batteries which were issued the Bombard. Before the formation of the RAF Regiment in 1942, British Army units were regularly tasked with defending the Royal Air Force's vital airfields. Some of these units were equipped with Bombards. Gordon Penter, a young soldier with 70th Battalion, The King's Regiment (Liverpool), was assigned to a Bombard team while stationed at RAF Leconfield in Yorkshire. Penter had a dim view of the weapon, noting that it was dangerous to use and quickly dispensed with (IWM 19769).

The Blacker Bombard also saw some limited use overseas, in North Africa. In January 1942, it was tested against a captured

Suffolk Home Guard members train with the Blacker Bombard, here mounted on its four-legged field mount. The No. 2 is loading an inert practice bomb. The No. 1 would then swing the weapon forward 90 degrees to engage the target. (© IWM H 12300)

PzKpfw IV medium tank, with Jefferis informing Lord Cherwell that on firing the first round at the PzKpfw IV's 30-degree frontal armour the 'complete right-hand section of vertical armour [was] blown inside tank … this appears satisfactory' (Jefferis to Lindemann, 01/02/42). The Eighth Army in North Africa was given a lower priority than units posted to East Asia, but still received some Bombards, which were deployed as temporary replacements for the 2-pdr anti-tank gun (Report on Visit to Middle East, 29mm Spigot Mortar, 20/03/42). In June 1942, the 23rd New Zealand Infantry Battalion was at least partially equipped with the new 29mm Spigot Mortar. Digging in near Minqar Qaim, the New Zealanders struggled to dig out the pedestal firing positions prescribed for their new weapons, which were viewed as rather bulky and clumsy and at their most effective at ranges of 100yd or less (Angus 1959: 145). Similarly, a month later, the 19th New Zealand Infantry Battalion reported that a neighbouring unit was practising with spigot mortars (Sinclair 1954: 269). How effective the Bombard was in North Africa is unclear, but an account from an unnamed officer of 4th Indian Division was printed in a Home Guard information circular of May 1943, recounting a defensive action on Miteriya Ridge during the battle of El Alamein in October 1942, in which the Bombards were 'used with good effect' in forward positions, going on to praise them as 'very inconspicuous, have a tremendous hitting power and are very simple to teach and learn' (Home Guard Information Circular No. 27, 12/05/43).

While the Bombard may have been effective, particularly for defensive actions, it was too cumbersome to equip the infantryman on the move. Soldiers still needed a weapon which was light enough to carry on the march and manoeuvrable enough to bring into action quickly, and it had to pack an effective punch. The PIAT represented a massive improvement in portability and effectiveness when compared to the infantry platoon's previous anti-tank weapon, the Boys.

A sergeant instructs a PIAT team of 1st Battalion, The Highland Light Infantry of Canada, on how to load a bomb into the PIAT, April 1944. (Library and Archives of Canada, MIKAN No. 3208268)

importance of good positioning of the PIAT was stressed, with instructors advising troops to find a concealed position, with a slit trench to be dug when fighting from a prepared position. The loading drill was then practised using a drill bomb, with the No. 2 practising loading the bomb into the PIAT's bomb support. How to aim at advancing, retiring and crossing targets was covered. Troops had to take into account the range to the target and choose either the top or bottom aperture of the rear sight depending on distance. To take on a moving target the trainees were advised to aim ahead of the enemy vehicle, but the most difficult part of hitting a moving target was continuing to lead it in the sights as the weapon was fired. Gunners were warned that the trigger pull was 'long and heavy' and taught to use two fingers rather than one. Immediate-action drills were also practised in case the weapon failed to launch its bomb or to re-cock. Firing of practice bombs took place on a 100yd range with the troops in full battle order. During practice firing, troops were advised to use some form of ear protection. No special ear protection was ever issued by the British Army, but cotton wool or 4×2in weapon-cleaning strips were recommended (Small Arms Training Vol. 1, Pamphlet No. 24, PIAT, 1943: 16).

The third and final lesson covered 'handling', with instructors discussing the use of the PIAT in the secondary light-mortar role for 'housebreaking', the desirability of shooting enemy AFVs from the flank or rear, and the importance of allowing a target to move within a close-enough range to ensure a 'kill' as ammunition in the field would often be limited. The class then practised elements of what they had learned before finally the secondary role was covered in more detail, with crews being taught how to set up the PIAT with its monopod extended, how to aim the weapon using the quadrant sight and white line painted along the top of the weapon, and how to fire the PIAT properly when using it as a light mortar – the No. 1 was taught to keep his head down while the No. 2 was to stand clear. They then – at least in theory – had the opportunity to practise firing in the secondary role, but this was often constrained by time and the availability of a firing range large enough to fire out to 350yd.

Despite troops being trained to strip the PIAT only as far as removing the cocking rod, spring and sleeve bolt, some keen soldiers went further and malfunctions due to 'excessive stripping' were reported (Army Council Instructions, 20/12/44). In December 1944, the General Staff was forced to issue a warning in the Army Council Instructions, telling troops that stripping beyond removing the working parts was prohibited and that 'stripping in excess of that laid down ... will be carried out be REME armourers' (ibid.).

Training on how the PIAT was to be used tactically in the field was laid out in the British Army's 1944 infantry manual on platoon tactics (Infantry Training, Part VIII, 1944). Essential reading for officers and NCOs, the manual explained how the PIAT could be used in a number of situations, ranging from ambushing enemy vehicles to assaulting urban areas. One of the uses covered was as a support weapon during an assault on an enemy pillbox. The platoon's 2in mortar would drop smoke on the target as the fire section laid down covering fire. The attacking section would then advance; the PIAT team would be attached to the attacking

Dutch troops fire inert practice bombs, painted white, from an early-model PIAT during manoeuvres in July 1943. (National Archives of the Netherlands, 2.24.01.05, 934-9309)

section and when they reached effective range they would break off and take up a position on the flank to engage the pillbox with direct fire. Once the enemy position had been captured, the PIAT team would move up and prepare for any possible enemy counter-attack (Infantry Training 1944: 83).

The PIAT could also be extremely useful when clearing buildings. The 1944 infantry manual explained how a platoon should clear a village. A fire section would take position to cover the main road through the village while the clearing group would attack the buildings from the rear. The PIAT team would accompany the clearing group and use the PIAT's 2.5lb explosive bomb to break into defended buildings. The manual explained that the PIAT was 'capable of penetrating a normal brick wall and produce considerable blast effect inside a room when penetrated' (Infantry Training 1944: 95). Once the PIAT had made a breach, the clearing group would rush into the house, clearing it with small arms and grenades.

The 1944 infantry manual also details the ideal hit-and-run ambush of enemy tanks and their supporting infantry. It explains that the platoon should establish three checkpoints, with men at each armed with No. 74 'Sticky Bomb' and No. 75 Hawkins anti-tank grenades. The enemy column would be allowed to reach the furthest checkpoint before the attack commenced. The attack would commence with smoke grenades being thrown ahead of the tanks and the fire sections opening fire on any supporting infantry. The PIAT team would be positioned at the centre checkpoint, with the manual explaining that the 'man with the P.I.A.T. will probably have time for one shot only' (Infantry Training 1944: 125). At the same time the other assault parties would run in with anti-tank grenades to attack the tanks. The whole platoon would then break off and fall back. While the manual suggested that the PIAT team might have time

FIRING THE PIAT

Whenever possible, the PIAT would be carried cocked but unloaded. Loading the PIAT was the job of the No. 2 (loader), who positioned himself to the left of the No. 1 (gunner) and loaded from the left with his right hand. Before loading a bomb into the PIAT it had to be prepared. The No. 2 would detach the fuze container, attached to the tail of the bomb, then remove the thimble from the bomb's nose and push the fuze into the bomb with the pointed end projecting outwards. He would then replace the thimble, turning it clockwise to secure it. This protected the fuze while he handled the bomb. He would then remove the muzzle plug from the bomb's tail tube and angle the bomb's nose down into the bomb-support tray through the front ring. Sliding the bomb forward until the tail could be lowered, he had to ensure that the loading clip slipped behind the two guide plates – this held the bomb in place, flush against the PIAT's housing and properly aligned with the spigot to prevent misfires. He then pushed the bomb down with the flat of his hand until the tail piece made contact with the bomb-support tray.

With the weapon cocked and the bomb loaded, the PIAT was ready to fire. The No. 1 lined up the PIAT on target, aligning the front sight post with one of the rear apertures; he then disengaged the safety, pushing it forward, and pulled the trigger.

As the trigger was pulled the sear holding the sleeve bolt back was lowered, and the spigot travelled forward within one-tenth of a second. The spigot travelled down its guide tube and projected out of the PIAT's housing and up the bomb's tail tube. Once the spigot reached its full length of travel, the firing pin at its tip detonated the propellant cartridge in the base of the bomb. The propellant gases then expanded, with the remains of the propellant cartridge creating a gas seal; the gases pushed against the head of the spigot, with the pressure pushing the bomb off the spigot and projecting it towards its target.

As the round began to travel forward, the loading clip, which was attached to the tail of the bomb by spring tension, detached and dropped through the opening at the bottom of the bomb-support tray, or was pushed out of the guides by the next bomb.

As the propellant pushed against the spigot, an equal and opposite reaction began pushing the PIAT's spring backwards. This rearward movement of the spigot and its sleeve bolt acted against the spring, re-cocking the weapon, with the trigger sear holding it in place. The spring mitigated the felt recoil of the bomb as it was

launched. When the PIAT was fired from a trench while standing, the recoil force was such that the No. 1 was advised to allow the recoil to swing his shoulder back about 6in. When firing from a prone position, the No. 1 was advised to fire with his feet together and his toes to the ground – somewhat similar to how Bren gunners were taught fire when prone. The operator was taught not to brace his feet against a solid object as the recoil would jar him and his back would take the brunt of the force.

Once the PIAT had been fired, and presuming the weapon had re-cocked itself, the No. 2 would come into action again, loading a fresh bomb. A rate of fire of five rounds per minute could be achieved by a well-trained crew. As was common in action the PIAT could be used by a single operator, loading and firing in his own time.

If the PIAT was not cocked or failed to re-cock after firing, the weapon had to be cocked manually. Cocking the PIAT was no simple feat, however, because it required the operator to overcome the spring's impressive strength in order to engage the sear. The operator first had to ensure the safety was set to 'fire' and that the sights were folded down to prevent snagging on equipment. In the standing position the weapon was stood vertically with the shoulder piece placed under the operator's feet, with a foot either side of the housing body/casing. The pistol grip and trigger guard were positioned to the right and the operator would then lean forward over the weapon, bending at the knees and grasping the back of the pistol grip or the trigger guard. To disengage the shoulder-piece locking catch, the body was pulled up slightly so it could be turned 45 degrees anti-clockwise. This disengaged the shoulder piece and cocking rod from the outer body of the PIAT. The operator then smartly straightened his knees, pulling the casing up about 12in against the pressure of the spring until the sear engaged and held the spring. The weapon was then placed on safe and the body lowered back down to the shoulder piece, and turned clockwise to lock it in place.

If the operator was under fire and could not stand up to cock the PIAT, the weapon could be cocked in the prone position. The operator would turn onto his side or back while remaining under cover and perform the same steps as when cocking in the standing position, but once cocked the shoulder piece could be turned back to the correct orientation with the feet.

for just one shot, a good team could certainly have managed two, perhaps three, during a short, sharp engagement.

A good example of this sort of ambush occurred during Operation *Market-Garden* in September 1944. On 22 September, Major Harry Parker of 5th Battalion, The Duke of Cornwall's Light Infantry, encountered a column of five German tanks, described as Tigers, at a crossroads south-west of Arnhem. Parker was able to prepare a textbook ambush, deploying his company's PIATs and strings of No. 75 Hawkins anti-tank grenades as anti-tank mines before lying in wait for the German column. When the action began, there was a large explosion; six PIAT rounds hit one tank, knocking it out, while a second vehicle struck the anti-tank mines and was also knocked out. A third tank tried to reverse out of danger, but hit more anti-tank mines before it stopped and was knocked out with a PIAT (Delaforce 2014: 143–44).

THE PIAT'S DEBUT: TUNISIA

During the latter stages of the Tunisian campaign (November 1942–May 1943), British troops began to be issued with the first PIATs. A small detachment from the British Army's elite unit of instructors, the Small Arms School Corps, demonstrated the new weapon to officers and men in early 1943.

Contemporary footage and reports suggest that the PIAT did see some action towards the end of the campaign. Footage filmed on 22 March 1943 by the War Office Film Unit shows men of 6th Battalion, The Royal Inniskilling Fusiliers, operating with a PIAT near Medjez el Bab (IWM AYY 372/1/2). One account of PIAT use emerged as part of recent research conducted by the Tank Museum at Bovington in Dorset. Eyewitness accounts and archival research combined to reveal that in April 1943, during the battle for Point 174, a ridge 10 miles north-east of Djebel Djaffa, Tiger '131' – the first Tiger I heavy tank to be captured intact by British forces – was engaged by not just a captured anti-tank gun and Churchill heavy infantry tanks but also by a lone PIAT. Sergeant John Oscroft of 2nd Battalion, The Sherwood Foresters, was ordered forward with a PIAT to engage the approaching Tiger, but his PIAT round glanced off the Tiger's hull. Oscroft was forced to take cover and only got one shot at the tank, which was eventually halted just yards from British positions. An anti-tank round jammed the Tiger's turret and the crew abandoned their vehicle. Tiger '131' was salvaged and quickly shipped back to the Britain for examination.

While the PIAT may have seen some use before the Axis surrender in North Africa in May 1943, it is unlikely it claimed any 'kills'. A pamphlet, published by ICI, claimed that the PIAT destroyed its first tank during fighting around Tunis, but a report written by the general staff of the First Army at the end of the Tunisia campaign in June 1943 contradicted this. The report stated that there was 'no evidence that this weapon [the PIAT] has as yet hit an enemy tank in motion. Trials show that this weapon will penetrate Pz Mks I–IV, but will not penetrate the Mk VI [Tiger I] except in the rear of the turret'; the report was also very blunt about the usefulness of the Boys Anti-Tank Rifle, calling for it to be 'abolished immediately' (1st Army Lessons Learnt in Tunisia Report, 16/06/43).

THE PIAT IN SICILY AND ITALY

The PIAT had its first confirmed successes during the Allied invasion of Sicily in July–August 1943. Some of its earliest victories came during Operation *Fustian*, the airborne assault on Primosole Bridge (13–16 July), which saw men of Britain's 1st Parachute Brigade and Commandos use PIATs to ambush a German column on 14 July. On 17 July, Canadian troops from 1st Battalion, The Hastings and Prince Edward Regiment, ambushed a German convoy travelling from Grottacalda. A PIAT bomb struck an enemy ammunition lorry which was also towing an 8.8cm gun. The bomb destroyed the lorry, immobilized the gun and killed the troops travelling in the vehicle. Buoyed by this early success, men of the regiment took on three German tanks which were defending the town of Valguarnera. Three of the PIAT rounds fired failed to explode when they hit the tanks, however, and the patrol was forced to retreat by fire from the tanks' machine guns. This was one of a number of incidents reported by troops of PIAT bombs bouncing off targets without detonating. On 26 July, Canadian infantrymen of 1st Battalion, The Edmonton Regiment, had more luck with their PIAT on the road to Nicosia, managing to destroy three enemy tanks, an SdAh 116 tank transporter and three accompanying lorries.

In early September 1943, the Allied invasion of mainland Italy began and the PIAT was soon in the thick of the action. The weapon would prove itself during the fighting in Italy, not only against armoured vehicles but also against pillboxes and during street fighting. During the campaign it became so prized for its 'housebreaking' abilities that it was dubbed by some the 'casa buster', a key tool in dislodging German strongpoints (Norton 1952: 495). At the beginning of the campaign, however, some units had not yet received PIATs. Peter Barrow of 2nd Battalion, The Lancashire Fusiliers, recalled finally being issued with the PIAT and training with it in the Italian hills (Sutton 2003: 109). In some cases there were still not enough PIATs available to equip units fully, however, and the 25th New Zealand Infantry Battalion received only five PIATs for the whole unit. Despite this the new weapons were soon put to good use and saw hard fighting over the next two years.

For most units the PIAT was still very much an untested weapon when it was issued in Italy. Some units put them to the test against abandoned Italian buildings. One such unit was the 28th (Maori) New Zealand Infantry Battalion, the official battalion history noting that while the PIAT's anti-tank capability remained untested, the weapon was highly effective against stone structures (Cody 1956: 323).

In December 1943, during fighting near Ortona, Sergeant Jean Paul Joseph Rousseau and his Canadian infantry platoon from Le Royal 22e Régiment engaged a PzKpfw IV medium tank. With covering fire from supporting platoons, Rousseau dashed across open ground, dropped to one knee and fired his PIAT at the tank at a range of just 35yd. His bomb struck the tank, penetrating its turret and detonating the ammunition inside, blowing the tank apart. The tank's crew were vaporized in the explosion and as many as 35 pieces of the destroyed vehicle were found scattered across the area after the battle. For his actions Sergeant Rousseau was awarded the Military Medal. This impressive success against a formidable enemy tank was quickly seized upon by a training memorandum published by 1st Canadian Division in an effort to reassure soldiers about the capabilities of the PIAT. The memorandum read: 'this quick, resolute and well thought out action demonstrated clearly that enemy tanks can be dealt with effectively by infantry men who have confidence in their weapons and the ability to use them' (Report No. 165 CMHQ: 68–69).

On 16 May 1944, during an attack on the Gustav Line as part of the Battle of Monte Cassino, a company of 2nd Battalion, The Lancashire Fusiliers, was forced to dig in and await support. The company took the brunt of a counter-attack by German armour with no supporting anti-tank guns available, instead being forced to rely on their PIATs. On his own initiative, Fusilier Francis ('Frank') Jefferson grabbed his PIAT and ran forward under fire to within 20yd of the lead vehicle, a StuG III self-propelled gun. Jefferson's first round struck just below the StuG III's gun, detonating ammunition inside the enemy vehicle. Jefferson fired while standing and later recalled how the force knocked him to the ground (IWM 1514). He reloaded and advanced on the second vehicle, which withdrew before Jefferson could engage it. His actions saved his company from being overrun and Jefferson was awarded the Victoria Cross for his gallantry (*The London Gazette*, 11/07/44).

Canadian infantry also used the PIAT in its secondary role as a light mortar to deal not just with stationary targets but also moving ones. On

24 May 1944, during the defence of the bridgehead over the Melfa River held by Canada's 2nd Battalion, The Westminster Regiment (Motor), Major John Keefer Mahony braved enemy fire to encourage his men and personally direct the fire of his company's PIATs. He ordered his PIAT teams to fire their weapons like mortars, hoping the high-angled fire would keep the approaching German tanks at bay. While none of the PIAT bombs found their mark, the tanks did eventually withdraw. Mahony was awarded the Victoria Cross for his direction of the Canadians' bridgehead defence (*The London Gazette*, 11/07/44). Lieutenant Alfred Reeves of 2nd Battalion, The King's Regiment (Liverpool), also put a PIAT to good use during an assault across the Gari River on the night of 11/12 May. Reeves's platoon was pinned down by fire from a German strongpoint in a house. Alone, he crawled forward

Italy, 1944 (overleaf)

A pair of British PIAT teams in action in Italy, 1943, engage a German Sturmgeschütz III self-propelled gun and its supporting infantry (out of view). On the left a PIAT team are using the weapon in its secondary, indirect-fire role to drop bombs on German infantry sheltering in the ruins of distant buildings. The No. 2 is preparing to load a bomb, but has noticed that the PIAT's spigot has not reset itself; the No. 1 will have to re-cock the weapon before they can fire again. This means he will either have to stand up and expose himself to enemy fire or roll over onto his back and awkwardly re-cock the weapon. The second team is directly engaging the approaching Sturmgeschütz III, with the No. 1 lining up his target while his No. 2 retrieves the next round from the bomb carrier for a follow-up shot. Providing the PIAT re-cocked itself, a team could fire up to 6rd/min.

50yd to within range of the house and opened fire, forcing the defenders to surrender. Lieutenant Reeves was awarded the Military Cross for his actions (*The London Gazette*, 17/04/45).

In Italy some units formed specialized tank-hunting platoons, each normally numbering about 20 men and equipped with four PIATs. Another Victoria Cross was won by a member of one of these tank-hunting platoons during fighting near the Savio River. On the night of 21/22 October 1944, 1st Battalion, The Seaforth Highlanders of Canada, spearheaded a crossing of the Savio which met with stiff resistance; the Canadian infantrymen were unable to summon armoured support due to flooding and were left with just their PIATs to defend themselves. The Germans counter-attacked in force with three Panther tanks and two self-propelled guns. Private Ernest Smith led a PIAT team forward across open ground, siting one team before retrieving another PIAT and advancing with his No. 2. His loader was wounded by machine-gun fire from one tank, but Smith managed to knock out the Panther with a single round. He then held off supporting enemy infantry with his Thompson submachine gun, protecting his wounded comrade. In the meantime the other PIAT team destroyed the two self-propelled guns and the German counter-attack broke up. For his bravery, Private Smith was awarded the Victoria Cross (*The London Gazette*, 19/12/44). During the same battle, Corporal William Crockett of 2nd Battalion, The Royal Fusiliers (City of London Regiment), led his platoon in house-to-house fighting. Crockett used his PIAT to break into three defended buildings before leading his men inside to clear them. This textbook example of 'housebreaking' with the PIAT earned Crockett the Distinguished Conduct Medal.

Another Military Medal was awarded to PIAT No. 1 Lance-Naik (Corporal) Ratan Singh Rana, of 3rd Battalion, 18th Royal Garhwal Rifles. On 14 December 1944, Ratan Singh was attached to a night patrol moving into Colve. When the patrol neared a house an enemy machine gun opened fire, wounding the patrol leader. Ratan Singh immediately brought his PIAT into action, silencing the machine-gun position. He then covered the patrol's retreat, continuing to engage with his PIAT.

During fighting along the Po River valley, PIATs were frequently used as light mortars. They proved to be very capable in this role, able to drop their bombs at a very close range on enemy trenches and dugouts. The war diary of 78th Division records that a huge number of bombs were fired, a single PIAT reportedly firing 600 rounds, in the light-mortar role, in just one day. While this is an extreme, it bears out the Ordnance Board's earlier concerns about the lifespan of the spring once PIATs were increasingly used as light mortars. Arthur John Wilton, an officer of 1st Battalion, The Royal Irish Fusiliers, recalled that during fighting in the Po Valley his men were often unable to call in an artillery barrage on nearby enemy positions because they were too close to their own lines. Instead his men frequently used their PIATs in the light-mortar role; where PIAT rounds hit an enemy dugout they caused substantial damage (IWM 33250). Sergeant Major Robbie Robinson, of

the same battalion, similarly recalled dropping PIAT bombs on targets along the Senio River, keeping up a continuous fusillade against enemy positions after dark. The PIAT bomb impacts on the rooves of dugouts created substantial shock waves and a considerable blast effect (Doherty 2015: 55).

As Allied forces pushed across the Senio in spring 1945, they encountered armoured resistance during a night attack on 10 April. A German Tiger heavy tank and several self-propelled guns counter-attacked and PIAT gunner Lance-Corporal R.J. Parker of the 21st New Zealand Infantry Battalion took on the Tiger, attacking it from its weakest point, the rear. Parker tried to fire twice but his PIAT failed to fire; it was only on his third attempt that he realized he had left the safety catch on. By the time he had this realization the Tiger had moved off down the road, leaving Parker to chase it; with the safety catch now disengaged he was able to knock the enemy tank out with his third attempt.

During one of the very last battles in Italy, Fusilier Dudley Cooper, serving with No. 2 Commando, put his PIAT to use both in the anti-tank and the light-mortar roles. During Operation *Roast*, a Commando attack across Lake Comacchio on the night of 1/2 April 1945, Cooper's unit was attacking across open ground when it came under fire. Cooper used his PIAT in its secondary role and engaged German machine-gun positions 300yd away. His No. 2 was killed and when an armoured counter-attack approached, Cooper manned his PIAT alone, twice having to make runs over open ground, under fire, for more bombs. He succeeded in halting the enemy vehicles before he ran out of ammunition and had to defend himself with his Colt M1911A1 pistol. For his actions Cooper was awarded the Military Medal.

ABOVE LEFT
Fusilier Francis ('Frank') Jefferson poses with his PIAT in front of the StuG III self-propelled gun he knocked out on 16 May 1944. (Sgt Menzies/Imperial War Museums via Getty Images)

ABOVE RIGHT
Private Stanley Rodgers, of 1st Battalion, 48th Highlanders of Canada, rests during a march to Rimini, Italy, in September 1944. The hefty 32lb PIAT must have been an unpleasant burden. Note the two slings to enable carrying the weapon over two shoulders. (Library & Archives Canada, MIKAN No. 3520465)

THE PIAT IN NORMANDY

In the hours before D-Day the gliderborne troops of D Company, 2nd Battalion, The Oxfordshire and Buckinghamshire Light Infantry, embarked on an audacious operation codenamed *Deadstick*. Major John Howard and his company were tasked with capturing and holding a pair of strategically vital bridges that crossed the Caen Canal and the Orne River. Once the bridges had been secured, Howard's men dug in and awaited reinforcements. With enemy armoured vehicles heard in the vicinity, Howard and his men managed to retrieve the PIATs stored in their gliders, only to find them badly damaged by the rough landings. Only one of D Company's PIATs was operational but it was quickly put to good use.

At about 0200hrs on 6 June, a column of German armoured vehicles from 21. Panzer-Division approached D Company's perimeter from the direction of Bénouville. Howard ordered the company's only PIAT to engage the first tank that came into range. Sergeant Martin Charles 'Wagger' Thornton was entrusted with the task of taking on the approaching armoured vehicles. With visibility very limited, Thornton spotted the slow-moving German armour and fired a PIAT round (IWM 11559). Howard recalled the anxious wait in the trenches; to his relief, the PIAT scored a direct hit on the leading tank, causing it to explode (Drez 1996: 112). The ammunition inside the tank detonated and the other enemy vehicles withdrew. Howard hadn't put all his faith in the PIAT and had also detailed soldiers to place No. 82 (Gammon Bomb) anti-tank grenades on the enemy vehicles (Drez 1996: 112).

There is some debate about what exactly Sergeant Thornton destroyed, with some accounts suggesting it was a PzKpfw IV medium tank while

A soldier fires his PIAT during fighting in Saint-Martin-des-Besaces, Normandy, on 1 August 1944. (© IWM B 8335)

others believed it was an older French tank. Regardless of the exact type of vehicle engaged by Thornton and his PIAT, he can be probably credited with D-Day's first armoured-vehicle 'kill'. For this and other actions during Operation *Overlord*, Sergeant Thornton was awarded the Military Medal.

At about 0900hrs on 6 June, Howard's men heard the sound of boat engines coming up the Orne River. Two German motor patrol boats fleeing No. 4 Commando's attack on Ouistreham soon ran into fire from paratroopers at the Bénouville bridges. Howard's men opened fire with a machine gun, prompting the Germans on the boat to return fire (Drez 1996: 114). Much to the amazement of some of his men, Corporal Claude Godbold, firing a PIAT, scored a direct hit on the lead boat's wheelhouse, causing the boat to run into the riverbank; its crew quickly surrendered.

Elsewhere in the hours before the main landings on Juno Beach, Canadian paratroopers put their PIATs to good use against an enemy pillbox. While attempting to secure the drop zone near Varaville, 1st Canadian Parachute Battalion was tasked with capturing a German bunker. The position proved to be stronger than the Canadians had anticipated and it was only through the use of their PIATs that they were able to knock out the pillbox and secure the position and the drop zone.

British and Commonwealth troops waded ashore on D-Day with their PIATs, but some men conveniently 'lost' their heavy weapons, abandoning what they foolishly thought of as unnecessary burdens. Despite this, the majority of men who retained their weapons made good use of them. On 6 June, the war diary for No. 4 Commando recorded that PIATs were used to destroy an enemy mortar position and a machine-gun post on the road into Ouistreham. Other elements of No. 4 Commando, under Captain Patrick Porteous, also attempted to use the PIAT on a German position inside a medieval tower being used as an artillery observation point. The PIAT round failed to penetrate the centuries-old masonry.

ABOVE LEFT
British troops advance in Normandy, August 1944. In the foreground is a lorry crammed with equipment including a pair of PIATs and ammunition carriers for the PIAT and the 2in mortar. (© Hulton-Deutsch Collection/CORBIS/Corbis via Getty Images)

ABOVE RIGHT
Men of No. 45 Commando wait to embark for the D-Day invasion. Interestingly, they are equipped with both a PIAT (on the left) and a Boys Anti-Tank Rifle (right). No. 45 Commando was part of 1st Special Service Brigade, which landed on Sword Beach. (© IWM H 39038)

According to Porteous, the walls were invulnerable, being 10ft thick (Ambrose 2014: 640).

The PIATs were not just in British and Canadian hands during the D-Day landings. During No. 4 Commando's landing on Sword Beach, a detachment of 177 Free French Commandos from 1er Bataillon de fusiliers marins commandos, commanded by Capitaine de Corvette Philippe Kieffer, was given the task of silencing the German strongpoint WN 10, a complex of bunkers including a 7.5cm gun, just outside Ouistreham. The strongpoint, built around the site of the old Riva Bella Casino, proved too strongly reinforced for the lightly equipped French Commandos to capture and they soon exhausted the ammunition for their two PIATs. Finally, with the assistance of a British Duplex Drive (amphibious) tank, Kieffer and his men silenced the German positions and captured the remains of WN 10.

Once men were ashore in force the PIAT played an important part in consolidating the Normandy beachhead, often providing troops with their only means of defence against enemy armoured vehicles. By 10 June, 9th Parachute Battalion had run out of ammunition for its 2in mortars and had resorted to using its PIATs in the light-mortar role. The brigade commander, Brigadier Stanley James Ledger Hill, recalled that the weapon was remarkably effective (IWM 12347).

Lance-Corporal George Price, a member of the anti-tank section of HQ Company, 12th Parachute Battalion, lost his PIAT and equipment during the D-Day airborne landings but managed to procure another from the airlanding battalions that followed them up. He recalled being given a PIAT and sent with two other soldiers of his section to take up position in the corner of a wood at Le Bas de Ranville; he noted that although his party might not have seemed to have posed much of a threat to enemy armour, the PIAT was certainly capable of disabling a tank if used appropriately (Neillands & De Normann 2012: 59–60).

Some PIAT teams even scored a number of Panther 'kills'. The first of these came on 8 June at Bretteville-l'Orgueilleuse, where Rifleman Joseph Lapointe of 1st Battalion, The Regina Rifle Regiment, knocked out a Waffen-SS Panther at close range. Lapointe and his No. 2 were positioned in a slit trench hidden behind a stone wall and as the Panther passed by he stood up and fired at a range of just 15yd. Despite a direct hit on the tank's thinner side armour it continued its attack. Lapointe fired two more rounds, the second of which caused the tank to crash into a wall where it detonated a cache of No. 75 Hawkins anti-tank grenades, destroying its right track and setting the vehicle on fire. For his action Lapointe was awarded the Military Medal.

As the Allied forces attempted to break out of their beachhead they entered Normandy's bocage country, a picturesque landscape characterized by farmland, orchards and sunken lanes lined by dense hedgerows which created a unique battlefield where opposing troops could be operating within yards of one another and not realize it. Company Sergeant Major William Rochester of 11th Battalion, The Durham Light Infantry, recalled a night action during Operation *Martlet* (25 June–1 July 1944) when the

enemy established a machine-gun position to enfilade the neighbouring British company, not realizing just how close Rochester's men were. It was decided to use one of the company's PIATs to silence the position before it did too much damage. Rochester and a PIAT team led by Private Stansfield, who had discovered the German position, waited until the gun opened fire. Aiming for the gun's flashes, Stansfield fired his PIAT, dropping a bomb directly on the machine gun. With the gun silenced the patrol moved up to survey the damage. Rochester recalled that the first hit had destroyed the machine gun and killed three members of the crew (IWM 14975).

During the fighting in bocage country the narrow twisting lanes and steep, wooded banks prevented the effective use of tank support and the battalion's anti-tank support weapons such as the 6-pdr gun. Troops fought from one hedgerow to the next and when enemy armoured vehicles or stubborn German defensive positions were encountered, their only effective weapon was the PIAT. Sergeant Albert Greatrix, with 1st Battalion, The Worcestershire Regiment, ran into one of these strongly entrenched positions in a sunken lane. Greatrix ran forward with a PIAT and fired at close range, destroying it. Greatrix was awarded the Military Medal for his bravery.

On 14 June, during fighting through the village of Verrières, south of Caen, infantrymen of 6th Battalion, The Durham Light Infantry, along with tanks from 4th/7th Royal Dragoon Guards, encountered a pair of Panthers from the Panzer-Lehr-Division. The British tanks knocked out the first and disabled the second, leaving Major John Mogg, of the Durhams, to destroy the immobilized, but still dangerous, Panther. He took two men and a PIAT forward, but after positioning the PIAT and ordering one of his men to prepare to fire, the soldier replied that he didn't know how to use the weapon, and the sergeant who had accompanied them was also unfamiliar with the PIAT. A frustrated

A PIAT team keeping their heads down in a corn field near Caen. Cover was essential if a slit trench could not be dug. It is possible to discern the markings on the face of the projectile, which suggest it is a Mk II bomb. (© IWM B 6185)

Mogg took the PIAT himself and, with a single round, destroyed the Panther, which burst into flames.

On 20 June, the daily news reports circulated among personnel of 43rd (Wessex) Division stated that during a German counter-attack conducted at night, two PIAT teams engaged a Panther, scoring three direct hits. Two rounds penetrated 'the side of the turret, while another rd [round] striking the base of the turret was deflected into the turret ring and prevented further traversing' (News Brevities, No. 5, 8th Bn, The Middlesex Regiment, 20 June 1944, WO 171/1341). The Panther began to retreat but was finally knocked out by No. 75 Hawkins anti-tank grenades. These actions show that even the Panther was vulnerable to the PIAT, which in numerous actions managed to knock out or force Panthers to retreat.

In late June, during fighting near Cheux, west of Caen, elements of 5th Battalion, The Duke of Cornwall's Light Infantry, were attacked by a platoon of German tanks. With the battalion HQ nearly overrun, Captain H. Jobson, OC D Company, gathered his company's three PIAT teams into a tank-hunting group, moved through an orchard and attacked the German tanks from behind. The PIAT teams went into action, knocking out three tanks and badly damaging another. Similarly, on 8 July, Lieutenant Vernon Kilpatrick of 1st Battalion, The Calgary Highlanders, led a patrol which knocked out three enemy tanks near Point 67 on Verrières Ridge.

The fighting around Hill 112, in mid-July, was extremely bitter, with tanks of 10. SS-Panzer-Division *Frundsberg* making a determined counter-attack. On 22 July, 5th Battalion, The Wiltshire Regiment, took some of the brunt during an attack on Louvigny and Company Sergeant Major Smith, who was bringing up ammunition in a Universal Carrier, saw one of the attacking tanks. He leapt out of his carrier with a PIAT, chased the enemy tank down and, in an impressive feat, used dead reckoning while firing from the hip to destroy his target.

As fighting in the bocage country continued the Allies launched Operation *Bluecoat* (30 July–7 August 1944), in an effort to break out. During *Bluecoat*, Company Sergeant Major J.E. Harrison of 4th Battalion, The King's Shropshire Light Infantry, successfully used a PIAT to destroy a Panther. According to his company commander, Harrison's first round bounced off the Panther's frontal armour as it retreated down the road, withdrawing some 70yd before coming to a halt. Harrison pursued the tank and soon discovered it behind a hedge, with the crew having dismounted (Thornburn 1990: 109). Harrison saw his opportunity and attempted to slide his PIAT though the hedge slowly, but the bomb fell out of his weapon – likely not secured by the loading clip. Harrison later told his company commander that he pulled the brushwood out of the way, pushed the PIAT through the hedge and pulled the trigger (Thornburn 1990: 109). He successfully destroyed the Panther, but was almost concussed by the explosion of his own bomb.

Not every engagement with a PIAT was successful, however. On 4 August, Captain Paul Stobart of 2nd (Armoured) Battalion, Irish Guards, engaged a Tiger II heavy tank near Estry, south-west of Caen,

CLANDESTINE USE OF THE PIAT

While the PIAT may not normally have fitted into SOE's clandestine operations, uses were found for the weapon. In the summer of 1944, a series of plans were drawn up for Operation *Foxley* – an attempt to assassinate Adolf Hitler – and the PIAT was one of the weapons discussed. It was one of the many methods that were initially suggested to kill Hitler, these including a 'sniper's rifle, PIAT gun (with graze fuze) or Bazooka, H.E. and splinter grenades, derailment and destruction of the Fuhrerzug by explosives; clandestine means' (TNA HS6/624). One plan suggested that Hitler might be targeted by a combined sniper/PIAT team while travelling from the railway station to Schloss Klessheim. Planning documents show that SOE severely overestimated the PIAT's ability, however, believing that it would be able to engage Hitler's car accurately at ranges of more than 300yd. Unsurprisingly, this option was abandoned for its lack of precision. An alternative plan called for a sniper to shoot Hitler as he took his morning stroll in the grounds of the Berghof. In the event that the sniper failed to kill Hitler, a second team would use a PIAT to destroy his car as it drove him back to the main house. The war ended before the plan could be put into effect, however.

The PIAT was dropped to Resistance fighters in substantial numbers. Operation *Jedburgh* saw specially trained, uniformed SOE and OSS operatives attached to French Resistance groups during the run-up to the Allied invasion. Their task was to help coordinate insurgent attacks on communications and transport infrastructure in the wake of the invasion. According to reports from the Allied Special Forces Headquarters to the Supreme Headquarters Allied Expeditionary Force, 288 PIATs had been dropped into France by June 1944. Between June and September 1944, more weapons were dropped with a further 1,161 anti-tank weapons (a mix of PIATs and American bazookas) delivered (Wieviorka 2013: 357). Michael Foot suggests that as many as 1,206 PIATs were dropped to various French SOE sections (Foot 2006: 424).

SOE dropped a variety of different equipment loads to guerrillas operating in occupied territories and ahead of advancing Allied armies. PIATs were typically dropped as part of a D Load, in 12 'C Type' containers, this load containing a mixture of small arms and either four bazookas with 56 rockets or one PIAT and 20 bombs.

British troops, including a captain, training Yugoslav partisans to operate the PIAT in 1944. (Author's Collection)

If the advancing Allied forces were composed of British and Commonwealth troops, they would be dropped British weapons, to simplify future logistics. Even when equipped with PIATs, members of the Resistance did not always have the training to use them. Jedburgh Team Aubrey attempted to ambush a German column in August 1944, but despite having four PIATs they were unable to utilize them properly and the operation became shambolic, descending into an 80-minute firefight with several Free French PIAT operators being injured by their own weapons. This is a clear example of the need for adequate training to operate weapons such as the PIAT properly, guerrillas with just hours of training being no match for regular forces in a pitched battle.

It was not just in Europe that the Jedburgh teams were operating. By 1944, teams deployed in Burma, operating ahead of Fourteenth Army, were leading bands of Burmese villagers carrying out intelligence-gathering and sabotage operations. The SOE's standard drop load, designed to equip 100 guerrillas, contained 54 carbines, 42 Sten submachine guns, 240 hand grenades, four Bren light machine guns, a Welrod silenced pistol and two PIATs. In addition to French and Burmese guerrillas, partisan forces across Europe – in Greece, Poland, Yugoslavia, Albania, Czechoslovakia and the Netherlands – were supplied with PIATs in small numbers.

firing three rounds at the front of the formidable vehicle with no visible effect. During operations in Normandy the PIAT undoubtedly proved itself on numerous occasions, but its limitations in range, effectiveness and ergonomics were also highlighted. As the Allies pushed east, the fighting continued to be fierce and the PIAT played an important part in many of the British and Commonwealth operations during late 1944 and spring 1945.

THE PIAT IN OPERATION *MARKET-GARDEN*

Following the breakout from the Normandy beachhead and the liberation of much of France, the Allies launched the most ambitious combined overland and airborne operation ever attempted. The goal was to use parachute and glider troops to capture a series of bridges from Eindhoven to Arnhem, with British XXX Corps racing 65 miles to Arnhem in the Netherlands to relieve the airborne troops at each of the bridges. The PIAT would play an important role in the ensuing battles, with elements of the British I Airborne Corps fighting for survival around Arnhem and Oosterbeek. As the platoon anti-tank weapon, the PIAT was, in many situations during the fighting in and around Arnhem, the airborne troops' primary weapon for taking on German armoured vehicles. Airborne divisions lacked the usual support and heavy weapons normally attached to infantry divisions and while anti-tank guns were successfully landed, when resupply drops failed and XXX Corps was unable to reach the airborne forces, the PIAT became their first and last line of defence.

By 18 September, Lieutenant-Colonel John Frost's men held the northern end of the Arnhem road bridge. Establishing an isolated defensive pocket around the approach to the bridge, Frost's men had a limited supply of ammunition and an even more limited supply of PIAT bombs and anti-tank-gun shells. Nevertheless, when an SS reconnaissance battalion, led by SS-Sturmbannführer Viktor-Eberhard Gräbner, attempted to force its way across the bridge at about 0900hrs on the 18th, the PIAT teams and gun crews opened up on the Waffen-SS armoured cars and half-tracks with devastating results. More than 20 vehicles created a maze of burning wreckage.

When the second wave of airborne troops landed on the evening of 18 September, they faced heavier resistance and some psychological warfare, with the Germans deploying a loudspeaker van to play messages warning that a Panzer division was advancing towards the Allied troops and calling on them to surrender. The messages were resolutely ignored and when the van got a little too close to British positions it was silenced by a direct hit from a PIAT bomb.

On the morning of 19 September, three British battalions attempted to break through to Frost's men at the bridge before dawn but found themselves trapped in a killing field under fire from German machine guns, anti-aircraft guns and self-propelled artillery. Once their attack broke up the British took up defensive positions, holding off a German tank counter-attack with the last of their PIAT ammunition. By about 1100hrs all PIAT ammunition had been exhausted and German armour penetrated the line held by 2nd Battalion, The South Staffordshire Regiment, and broke up the battalion into pockets. Meanwhile, inside the Arnhem perimeter Private Robert Lygo, a PIAT No. 1 with 2nd Battalion, The Parachute Regiment, single-handedly beat off an attack by three German armoured cars and later destroyed an enemy armoured vehicle. Lygo was awarded the Military Medal for his actions.

By 20 September, ammunition for Frost's PIATs was scarce. In Oosterbeek, Major Robert Cain of 2nd Battalion, The South

Staffordshire Regiment, was instrumental in bolstering the hard-pressed British perimeter against repeated German attacks during the afternoon. When self-propelled guns threatened his company's position, Cain used a PIAT in a textbook example of the weapon's secondary role as a mortar. Firing at high elevation, Cain dropped bombs on a self-propelled gun which was positioned in an enfilading position on the other side of a house. The bombs, fired at a near-vertical angle, passed over the house and landed near the enemy vehicle (*The London Gazette*, 31/10/44). A German shell hit the building's chimney, wounding Cain and killing his spotter before he could zero in on his target. Later that day, Cain engaged two enemy tanks, halting one with a PIAT bomb; when he fired a second to ensure the tank had been knocked out the bomb prematurely exploded just as it left the weapon. Staff Sergeant Richard Long, of the Glider Pilot Regiment, saw the explosion and described how Cain appeared to throw the PIAT in the air and fall backwards, his face badly wounded with small metal fragments from the explosion. While Cain was being treated, word arrived from forward positions that German heavy tanks were approaching. Cain immediately grabbed another of the company's PIATs and began stalking the tanks. He hit the first tank but was wounded again by machine-gun fire and flying masonry. He continued firing, scoring several more hits, until a 75mm howitzer was brought up to finish off the immobilized tank. The following day he took on three more enemy tanks, firing either at near-point blank range or leaving cover to engage the enemy, 'with complete disregard for his

ABOVE LEFT
Specially designed load-bearing kit was developed for airborne troops to carry between five and seven bombs along with the PIAT itself and possibly a personal weapon. This would in theory allow troops to carry more ammunition from the landing zone. This equipment was trialled by the Airborne Forces Development Centre in 1944, but seemingly not adopted. (Airborne Assault, Parachute Regiment Museum, www.paradata.org.uk)

ABOVE RIGHT
A German photograph of captured British ordnance in Oosterbeek, including several mortars and a PIAT. (Bundesarchiv Bild 101II-M2KBK-771-13 Foto: Höppner, Willi)

personal safety' (*The London Gazette*, 31/10/44). By 25 September, Cain's men had run out of PIAT ammunition and he personally began using a 2in mortar at close range. Awarded the Victoria Cross for his gallantry, Major Cain was the only one of five VC recipients at Arnhem to survive the battle.

Elsewhere on 20 September, another supreme act of bravery took place at Oosterbeek, where Private Walter Landon of 21st Independent Parachute Company ran out into the open to get a shot at a marauding German self-propelled gun. Landon succeeded in disabling the enemy vehicle with his PIAT, but as he returned to cover he was mortally wounded.

The street fighting in Arnhem and Oosterbeek also saw the PIAT used against buildings, as laid out in the 1944 infantry manual, to blow holes in walls. Sergeant Des Page, a glider pilot, recalled using PIAT bombs to clear German snipers, who had just shot a medic in the knee, from their positions in some houses. Lieutenant John Stevenson of 156th Parachute Battalion wrote in his diary that when the Germans pushed them out of Oosterbeek's bakery, they were forced to try to knock it down, recalling that he fired the PIAT at a range of only 50yd, blowing a large hole in the bakery wall (Beevor 2018: 269). Elsewhere within the Oosterbeek perimeter, Corporal James Swan of 1st Battalion, The Border Regiment, spotted a German machine-gun crew setting up in a small depression in the ground roughly 50yd ahead of the British positions. Corporal Swan was going to shoot the gunner with his No. 4(T) sniping rifle, but before he could do so, Private Davis loaded his PIAT and fired, killing the entire machine-gun crew.

On 24 September, Private Frank Dixon, a platoon cook, took on an enemy tank with a couple of scrounged-up PIAT bombs. Dixon crept through some bushes until he was within 50yd of the tank. He managed to hit it with his first shot, and the vehicle's crew were cut down as they tried to escape its burning remains.

By the time the fighting around Arnhem and Oosterbeek ended on 26 September, the British airborne troops had long since run out of PIAT ammunition and had held on seven days longer than they had expected to. Major Richard Lonsdale, OC 11th Parachute Battalion, wrote an after-action report laying out operational failures but also praising the PIAT. He noted that the PIATs 'proved of immense value' and that 'the tragedy of the operation was the shortage and towards the end the complete lack of them. Time without number the cry was "Give me the PIATs and we'll stay until Christmas"' (11 PARA Report on Operations, 21/10/44).

THE PIAT IN NORTH-WEST EUROPE AFTER OPERATION *MARKET-GARDEN*

From the autumn of 1944 onwards the Allied forces fought their way across North-West Europe, liberating Belgium and the Netherlands and crossing the Rhine River into Germany. The battle of Geel in September 1944 involved British troops of XXX Corps fighting near the hamlet of

Stokt. Men of 8th Battalion, The Durham Light Infantry, ran into a Jagdpanther tank-destroyer on 12 September and, with no other support available, Sergeant Joseph Middleton crawled to within 15yd of the vehicle and hit it with a single PIAT round before opening fire on the supporting infantry with his Sten submachine gun. Middleton was awarded the Military Medal for his actions. Not every direct hit was a 'kill', however. During fighting near Elst on the night of 24/25 September, Private Reginald Lugg of 1st Battalion, The Worcestershire Regiment, engaged and hit a German heavy tank with his first shot, but it took four more rounds to destroy the vehicle.

As 4th Battalion, The Royal Welch Fusiliers, fought through the Dutch village of Wintelre on 21 September, Lance Sergeant William Hindley's Carrier section came under heavy fire from German machine guns and *Panzerfäuste* in several houses. Hindley moved his section forward to within 50yd of the houses and systematically levelled each building with PIAT fire.

Fighting near Rischden, on the German border, in November 1944, saw Sergeant Charles Drew of 1st Battalion, The Worcestershire Regiment, engage a counter-attacking German tank at the extreme range of 300yd. Out of range for engaging the tank directly and with his company taking heavy casualties, Drew began firing a PIAT at a high angle – like a mortar. His first two rounds missed but his third miraculously struck the top of the tank's turret and set the vehicle on fire. While this was not the standard method of engaging a tank with the PIAT, the bomb penetrated its thinner roof armour and knocked it out.

At the end of 1944, the Allies began operations to liberate the Scheldt and re-open Antwerp to shipping. During the battles that followed, the PIAT was used numerous times against German positions and vehicles. Canadian Private J.C. Carrière of 1st Battalion, Le Régiment de Maisonneuve, won the Military Medal by crawling forward down a water-filled ditch and knocking out a 20mm gun, which was harassing Canadian positions, with a PIAT. Sergeant E.J.

ABOVE LEFT
Photographed in November 1944, this soldier of 5th Battalion, The Duke of Cornwall's Light Infantry, carries a PIAT over one shoulder and a rifle over the other, a combined weight of just over 40lb. (© IWM B 11928)

ABOVE RIGHT
British troops in action in the streets of Geilenkirchen, near the Dutch–German border, in December 1944. The PIAT No. 1 is also armed with a Sten Mk III submachine gun. (© IWM BU 1335)

Laloge of 1st Battalion, The Calgary Highlanders, won the Distinguished Conduct Medal for breaking up an enemy counter-attack with his platoon's PIAT.

Stalking tanks with the PIAT was no easy mission. While involved in street fighting in the village of Bure in Belgium during the Battle of the Bulge on 3 January 1945, Corporal David Robinson of the Anti-Tank Platoon, HQ Company, 13th Parachute Battalion, was ordered to take his PIAT and two men to destroy a Tiger tank which was in a hull-down defensive position with only its turret visible. Robinson crossed through back gardens past sheds, hedges and chicken runs before being spotted and pinned down. Grabbing his PIAT, Robinson ordered his men to retire and sprinted back to the Allied lines. Major Jack Watson, OC A Company, won the Military Cross during the fighting for personally directing his company's PIATs and luring a Tiger into range of a PIAT by deliberately drawing attention to himself.

THE PIAT ON THE EASTERN FRONT

The PIAT saw much less use on the Eastern Front despite the fact that the Soviet Union had been sent a significant quantity of the weapons. By March 1944, 800 PIATs and 85,000 PIAT bombs had been sent to Russia under Lend-Lease agreements; by the end of the war that number had risen to 1,000 PIATs and 100,000 bombs (Hansard, 10/05/44). There is no evidence to suggest that the PIATs sent to the Soviet Union were used in action.

The PIAT was, however, used extensively by the Polish Home Army in the desperate fighting during the Warsaw Uprising in August 1944. When the Uprising began on 1 August, the Home Army in Warsaw had fewer than 50 PIATs in its arsenal, otherwise relying upon homemade *filipinki* petrol bombs as the primary anti-tank weapon. The RAF flew a series of sorties in an effort to supply the Home Army in Warsaw, but

without Soviet assistance the uprising stood little chance. As Warsaw became a ravaged landscape of rubble and damaged buildings, the fierce street-to-street and house-to-house fighting continued. By 17 August, more than two weeks into the fighting, just 70 PIATs and 1,700 bombs had been supplied to the Poles. By 12 September, and despite logistical difficulties and Soviet obstinacy, the Allies had dropped 250 PIATs into Warsaw; it is difficult to estimate just how many of these reached Polish hands.

Zbigniew 'Deivir' Czajkowski, a corporal and patrol leader with the Polish Home Army's 'Parasol' scout battalion, described using a PIAT against a German tank in his diary. Positioned on the second floor of a building, Czajkowski saw the tank approaching; the PIAT operator next to him was about to fire when he realized he hadn't fuzed the bomb. Czajkowski took the PIAT from him, primed the bomb and fired, missing the tank's turret. The PIAT's original operator snatched it back and began to aim when Czajkowski realized why he had missed – he was firing the weapon from the second floor. Once he adjusted the angle to aim, he successfully hit the tank (Czajkowski 2012: 99).

The PIAT gave the besieged soldiers of the Polish Home Army a much-needed weapon capable of taking on armoured vehicles and strongpoints, but a few dozen PIATs could not even the odds and slowly the Polish perimeter shrank. As the survivors of the Uprising attempted to escape through Warsaw's sewers, exhaustion took its toll. Czajkowski described in his diary how he and his squad shared the duties of carrying the precious PIAT. Even sharing the load, in such cramped conditions the weapon was very difficult to carry (Czajkowski 2012: 131). When the next man in the column refused to take the heavy weapon, Czajkowski turned and dropped the PIAT at his feet and threatened him with his MP 40 submachine gun. The man quietly picked up the PIAT. Czajkowski made it to safety just before the Polish surrender on 2 October.

THE PIAT IN THE FIGHT AGAINST JAPAN

The PIAT also made its mark in the struggle against the forces of Imperial Japan in Asia and the Pacific. Seeing use with British and Commonwealth troops in Burma, the PIAT engaged not just Japanese tanks but also bunkers, boats, lorries and trains.

By late 1943, Indian Army battalions were issuing the PIAT at a similar rate to their British counterparts, with Indian light infantry and reconnaissance battalions equipped with four while the motor battalions had 11 and machine-gun battalions fielded up to 15. Corporal George MacDonald Fraser of 9th Battalion, The Border Regiment, took part in the Burma campaign; he was put in charge of a PIAT while on detached duty. While he had been trained in Britain in how to use the PIAT, he had never had the chance to fire the weapon. He fired his first practice round at a captured Japanese bunker near a small Burmese village. In his memoir, he describes being watched by a section of Burmese irregulars as he fired at the bunker 80yd away. He describes how his first shot fired from a PIAT was earsplittingly loud, with fierce recoil; he missed his target by about 30yd. Fraser managed to hit the bunker with his second round, leaving nothing but a cloud of black smoke where it had once been. He described the PIAT as being akin to many British inventions, in that it looked strange and dangerous to the user, but it worked (Fraser 1992: 328). As the local PIAT specialist, Fraser joined an ambush of Japanese troops who were attempting to retreat on a river barge, taking with him a PIAT and just ten bombs. Fraser and his comrades lugged the PIAT across 8 miles of paddy and jungle. Fraser described some of the difficulties of carrying the heavy weapon across difficult jungle terrain, with the weapon getting caught on vegetation and the brush too dense to share the load between two. Despite changing bearers regularly, within 20 minutes Fraser felt the PIAT was wearing furrows in his shoulders, while his back and legs ached from the strain (Fraser 1992: 328).

When the members of the ambush party finally reached their positions they were exhausted and Fraser realized he had not cocked the PIAT. He remembered his drill and described how he rolled over and successfully cocked the weapon. He gives a very vivid account of using the PIAT against a very difficult target, a moving raft-like river barge. After firing his first shot he rolled into cover and counted, waiting for the explosion. Missing with his first shot, his No. 2 loaded another round. Fraser lined up his sights, aiming just behind the barge's bow. Firing again, he was struck on the chin by the PIAT's recoil; he missed again, having to re-cock the PIAT on his back while in the prone position. His No. 2 reloaded and told him where his shots had fallen; with his third shot he hit the barge, splitting the raft into chunks of bamboo, sinking it in moments (Fraser 1992: 328).

Major-General Orde Wingate was reportedly an admirer of the PIAT and the firepower it offered to soldiers operating deep behind enemy lines. In his training notes, written in late 1943 to outline how he wanted his forthcoming second incursion into Burma to proceed, he made frequent mention of the PIAT and its use in ambushes and raids against Japanese infrastructure. During the campaign, Operation *Thursday*, the PIAT was used as Wingate had envisaged. During a number of raids on Japanese transport centres the Chindits (or Long Range Penetration Groups) used the PIAT and flamethrowers to destroy Japanese trains and lorries. Lieutenant Richard Rhodes James, attached to the Chindits, recalled in his memoir his men's favourable impression of the new anti-tank weapon and praised its devastating effect on Japanese tanks (Rhodes James 1980: 103).

As encounters with tanks were far less likely in Asia and the Pacific than in Europe, British and Commonwealth forces sought other uses for their PIATs. Bunker-busting seemed like an ideal use and the PIAT's effectiveness against Japanese field fortifications and bunkers was the subject of reports by both the United States and Australia. Upon investigating the PIAT's ability to penetrate earth and bamboo emplacements, however, the results were not as promising as expected. The US Infantry Board at Fort Benning, Georgia, carried out testing against a recreated Japanese bunker using earth and hard and soft woods. The report from October 1943 noted that while the PIAT had accuracy comparable to that of the M9A1 rifle grenade, its penetration was superior when fired against solid targets. The PIAT was, however, found to be unsuited to jungle work as it had to be fired from the prone position and so might not clear ground vegetation. The report also suggested that almost 100 per cent of the rounds fired failed to detonate when striking soft earth. It is worth noting that the report was written before the improved No. 426 graze fuze was introduced. The Infantry Board's report concluded that the PIAT was 'not a suitable jungle warfare weapon' (Report of the US Infantry Board, No. 1532, Weapons For Jungle Warfare, 30/10/43: 2-5).

Australian testing of the PIAT began in May 1943, with demonstrations to various departments and units taking place in June and July. Interestingly, the Australian military altered the name of the PIAT, often referring to it as the Projector, Infantry, Tank-attack or PITA. The earliest reference to the PITA I have come across dates from June 1943, when the terms PITA and PIAT appear to have been largely interchangeable. I have been unable to ascertain why exactly this alternative nomenclature was adopted. The PITA nomenclature extends to an official Australian Military Forces small arms training pamphlet, Vol. 1 No. 16, as well as a parts-list pamphlet published by the Australian Army in May 1945, which details the parts for an unaltered early-production version of the PIAT.

By December, Australian Army troops at the New Guinea Force training school had tested the PIAT against a replica Japanese earthwork bunker. It was found that 'the PITA is NOT a suitable weapon' for use against Japanese field defences because it had to strike the target cleanly and the target also had to have a sufficiently hard surface to detonate the bomb (User Trials – Projector Infantry Tank Attack, Appendix A, New Guinea Force, 27/01/44). The nature of the PIAT's shaped-charge projectile meant that the fragmentation of the projectile itself was minimal and when impacting on wood or earth its effect was severely limited. Results found that the majority of the bombs fired against the bunker

Members of an Australian PIAT team from 2/10th Battalion take cover behind a tree during the battle of Balikpapan, July 1945. They are equipped with an early-pattern PIAT without quadrant sights or adjustable front monopod. The No. 2, armed with an SMLE Rifle No. 1 Mk III, has two three-round bomb carriers on his back. (AWM 111069)

failed to detonate or ricocheted, with only a handful of successful detonations which created 2in-diameter holes, but the blast effect inside the bunker was minimal. The New Guinea Force's testing found that 'these weapons, using the present type of fuze are of a value only when AFVs are likely to be encountered'; this, however, was a rare prospect in New Guinea (User Trials, New Guinea Force, 27/01/44). As a result it was suggested that forces in New Guinea issue the PIAT at a rate of one per company, rather than one per platoon. Testing by elements of Australian II Corps and 7th Australian Division produced similar results, with the report noting that 'it is not considered that the PITA is of any use except against armour' (User Trials, New Guinea Force, 27/01/44). Despite this, on 4 May 1945, during the battle of Tarakan – part of the Allies' campaign to retake Borneo – Trooper R. Nugent of the Australian 2/4th Commando Squadron, armed with a PITA, successfully destroyed a Japanese concrete bunker which dominated the summit of Tarakan Hill.

Contemporary photographs show that as late as July 1945, Australian troops were still equipped with the initial-production PIATs, lacking the adjustable front monopod, mortar sight and flat-faced butt. Similarly, later photographs of the Commonwealth Occupation Forces in Japan show Australian troops armed with the same early-pattern PIATs, indicating that their PIATs were neither replaced nor upgraded. The Australian military began removing their remaining PIATs from service in the late 1950s, like Britain, replacing them with the 3.5in rocket launcher.

In March 1944, Japanese forces invaded north-eastern India with Allied forces desperately scrambling to counter the invasion. During

Private T.E. Hannon of Australia's 61st Battalion struggles to cock his PIAT in long grass, the effort of doing so evident in his expression. (AWM 067025)

fighting near Nippon Hill, east of Imphal, Japanese light tanks played havoc with Allied positions which could not be supported by heavier British tanks. On 11 April, PIAT teams from 1st Battalion, The Devonshire Regiment, were sent forward but the terrain was so open that they could not get within range of the enemy tanks and were forced back (IWM 19771). A more successful engagement took place on 12 June during fighting around Imphal, when Rifleman Ganju Lama, a PIAT No. 1 of 1st Battalion, 7th Gurkha Rifles, single-handedly knocked out two of five Japanese tanks attacking near the village of Ningthoukhong. According to his VC citation, Ganju Lama crawled forward under heavy enemy fire and on his own initiative began firing his PIAT at the enemy tanks. Eventually closing to within 30yd, Lama continued his attack despite suffering a broken left wrist, a wounded right hand and a wound to his leg. He managed to destroy two Type 97 ShinHoTo Chi-Ha medium tanks; breaking up the Japanese attack, he then engaged their retreating crews with grenades (*The London Gazette*, 5/09/44). A month earlier, on the Tiddim Road, Lama had been awarded the Military Medal for stalking and destroying another Japanese tank with his PIAT.

India, 1944 (overleaf)

Here, a Gurkha PIAT operator engages Japanese armour at close range. He has already hit one Type 97 ShinHoTo Chi-Ha medium tank, despite his No. 2 being seriously wounded. Similarly, Rifleman Ganju Lama of 1st Battalion, 7th Gurkha Rifles, engaged an approaching platoon of Japanese light tanks attacking near the village of Ningthoukhong on 12 June 1944, during the battle of Imphal. Ganju pressed his attack alone, taking out two Type 97 tanks despite being wounded in his arms and leg, all the time under Japanese machine-gun fire. After knocking out the tanks he attacked the surviving crews with hand grenades as they retreated. For his gallantry Rifleman Ganju Lama was awarded the Victoria Cross.

THE PIAT AFTER 1945

After the war the PIAT continued on in service, with a generation of young National Servicemen also becoming familiar with this unusual weapon. Despite this, the PIAT saw limited use in Britain's post-colonial operations in Malaya and Kenya, for there was little call for an anti-tank weapon when fighting insurgents. By the time the Korean War erupted in June 1950, the PIAT was largely considered obsolete. In 1949, it had been acknowledged by the Director of Artillery (Small Arms) that the PIAT would not be manufactured again. As a result, British and Commonwealth forces deployed with the United Nations forces in Korea were largely equipped with the American M20 3.5in rocket launcher, replacing the PIAT in kind, with one issued to each platoon. Some PIATs appear to have made it to Korea with rear-echelon units such as the Royal Engineers and Royal Electrical and Mechanical Engineers. Canadian and Australian forces in Korea were also largely equipped with the American rocket launchers, with the Canadians also abandoning their 2in and 3in mortars for the American 60mm and 81mm mortars. Not only was the M20 a more effective weapon, its wider issue among United Nations forces simplified logistical considerations.

The PIAT continued to see active service around the world in the hands of Greek, French, Dutch, Indian, Pakistani and Israeli soldiers. The Greek Civil War, which began in 1946, saw an influx of arms and support from both Britain and the United States. As a result the PIAT was used by elements of both the Greek National Army and the Communist guerrillas. In August 1949, during Operation *Pyrsos*, the last battle of the Greek Civil War, government forces captured ten PIATs from the guerrillas.

The PIAT also saw extensive service during post-colonial campaigns fought by various European countries, including the Netherlands and France. During the Indonesian War of Independence (1947–49), Dutch troops fighting Indonesian nationalists also deployed PIATs. At the end of World War II the PIAT became the Dutch Army's primary infantry anti-tank weapon, with a version of the British Army's manual for the PIAT translated into Dutch in August 1945. During World War II the Royal Netherlands Motorized Infantry Brigade, which had fought as part of the British Army, had been equipped with British weaponry, including the PIAT. Dutch troops fighting in the Dutch East Indies used the PIAT as an indirect-support weapon. The first Dutch division to arrive in the Dutch East Indies after the end of Japanese occupation in 1946 was equipped with no fewer than 421 PIATs. While the conflict ended with Indonesian independence in December 1949, the PIAT continued on in Dutch service into the early 1950s, with Dutch forces transitioning, like many former PIAT users, to the American M20 'Super Bazooka'.

Various photographs taken during the First Indochina War (1946–54) show French forces equipped with surplus British PIATs. Some show the weapons in mortar pits, being used as light mortars, while others show infantry carrying them in the field. One fascinating post-war French use of the PIAT is confirmed by a number of photographs of French river patrol boats. The French Navy operated a flotilla of landing craft and

patrol boats along the rivers of Vietnam, some of which were mounted with a pair of PIATs, one on either side, for use against Việt Minh shore targets. French forces also encountered PIATs during the 1954–62 Algerian War, with several being captured from Algerian guerrillas during operations. In February 1958, the 1er Régiment Etranger de Parachutistes recovered a PIAT and 24 projectiles, along with over 150 grenades, eight machine guns, 116 rifles and 60,000 rounds of ammunition, during fighting in the Algerian mountains (Balazuc 2015: 232).

One of the most prominent post-war conflicts in which the PIAT was involved was the 1947–49 Arab-Israeli conflict. The PIAT was one of the few anti-tank weapons which the Jewish paramilitary forces, the Haganah, could call upon to face Arab armoured vehicles. To the Haganah, and later the Israel Defense Forces, the PIAT was in some cases the only defence against superior Arab armour. As the war began, outlying Israeli settlements came under attack; many of these settlements, such as Kfar Etzion, Kfar Darom, Yad Mordechai and Negba, had only a single PIAT to defend themselves. On 19 May 1948, during an Arab attack on Israeli positions in Jerusalem, near the Mandelbaum Gate, Jordanian troops supported by armoured cars were beaten back by members of the Haganah with a PIAT and petrol bombs, while on 22 May, another PIAT team knocked out two more armoured cars attacking the Notre Dame compound (Morris 2008: 214–16). Later fighting in the south saw the Hanegev Brigade launch jeep raids behind Egyptian lines; these raiding jeeps were equipped with German machine guns and PIATs.

During fighting around Degania Alef on 20 May, Syrian tanks briefly broke through the Israeli perimeter until a PIAT gunner, Yitzhak Eshet, engaged the lead light tank, a Renault R 35. Eshet fired from a slit trench at a range of 40yd, but his first round failed to explode. He was

An American M20 'Super Bazooka', courtesy of the SASC Infantry Weapons Collection Trust. A rocket launcher which split into two parts for transport, it was significantly lighter and more effective than the PIAT. (Author's photograph)

A Dutch soldier uses his PIAT as a light mortar, with its fully extended monopod leaning on a rock for extra elevation, in Indonesia. On the ground next to him is another British weapon, a Sten Mk II submachine gun. (H. Wakker, National Archives of the Netherlands, Fotocollectie Anefo)

Hersh Makowski, a former member of the British-trained and -equipped Jewish Brigade, was the only member of the Alexandroni Brigade to have experience with the PIAT. As such he became chief instructor and explained its operation to other members of the brigade. (United States Holocaust Memorial Museum 74692)

forced to fire his second shot from the hip, this time disabling the approaching tank (Morris 2008: 256).

In July 1948, Israeli forces counter-attacked Egyptian forces in in the Negev desert. During the battle of Karatiyya, Egyptian tanks pushed into the village. Armed with a PIAT and just two bombs, Sergeant Ron Feller crawled along a low cactus fence line until he was within 25yd of the Arab tanks. His painstaking crawl took him 35 minutes, but once within range he pushed his PIAT through the cactus and fired. His first shot missed and he had to re-cock the PIAT under fire. His second shot disabled the tank and the rest of the Egyptian armour retreated. Feller received the Hero of Israel award – at the time Israel's highest military honour – for his actions (Gilbert 1998: 220). Once again, the PIAT gave an under-equipped force a fighting chance in the face of seemingly overwhelming odds. By the time the Israel Defense Forces took part in the Suez Crisis (October–November 1956), the PIATs had been replaced by American rocket launchers.

Arab-Israeli War, 1948 (opposite)

Members of the Haganah defend a hastily constructed roadblock, consisting simply of piles of rocks, across a road leading to a kibbutz. The defenders are engaging an approaching Syrian tank, a surplus French R 35. In the distance an Israeli machine-gun team armed with a war-surplus German MG 34 general-purpose machine gun opens fire, while the assistant gunner prepares a Molotov cocktail. As a PIAT team defending the second roadblock opens fire, the team's No. 2 searches for another round in the empty bomb carrier. The few PIATs possessed by the Haganah were distributed in ones and twos to the units defending isolated kibbutzim, as well as to those fighting in cities such as Jerusalem. The PIATs were found to be more than adequate, scoring numerous victories during the fighting; they represented the only real infantry anti-tank weapon possessed by the Israelis.

IMPACT
Punching above its weight

THE SOLDIERS' VERDICT

Perhaps the best way to gauge a weapon's impact and effectiveness is to examine what the soldiers who used the weapon thought of it. Over the years the PIAT has gained a poor reputation but from contemporary and later recollections it is clear that while some soldiers had little confidence in it, others believed it to be an effective weapon.

While the individual impressions of soldiers who encountered and used the PIAT can only be considered subjective, they do provide us with an important insight into understanding how the PIAT performed in action. Their opinions depended largely on a number of factors, including the amount and quality of the training they received – ranging from a proper course with the chance to fire the weapon, to seeing brief demonstrations only. They may have seen the weapon fail in action or even simply had to carry its 32lb hulk on a long route march.

We have already seen that 11th Parachute Battalion's commanding officer, Major Richard Lonsdale, was impressed by the PIATs' performance during the fighting around Arnhem. From combat experience he believed them to be invaluable, noting that 'at short range they are a good and destructive weapon' (11 PARA Report on Operations, 21/10/44). Similarly, William Carter, another Arnhem veteran with 1st Battalion, The Parachute Regiment, felt the PIATs deployed at Arnhem were effective in the anti-tank role (IWM 15534).

A BBC Radio broadcast from Normandy on 22 June 1944, during the bitter and prolonged fighting in the bocage country in the weeks after D-Day, also gives us some insight into the general opinion of the PIAT. BBC war correspondent Robert Dunnett described the usefulness of the PIAT during the broadcast:

If ever an infantry weapon has justified its existence, that weapon is the PIAT … Every day one hears of German tanks knocked out or at least immobilised, by PIATs. In copses, behind hedges, among groups of ruined buildings, in any sort of position where our men can find cover enough to creep up to them with their PIATs. Our infantry swear by the PIATs. (Quoted in ICI Pamphlet on PIAT, 1945)

Another interesting insight into the soldier's opinion of the PIAT comes from a series of 'Battle Experience Questionnaires' completed by Canadian officers who served in the Mediterranean and North-West Europe. The questionnaire asked officers for their opinions on the weapons they and their men used. One question asked if they considered any weapon 'outstandingly effective': the PIAT received more positive responses than any other weapon, with the Bren gun coming a respectable second. An impressive 74 respondents, out of more than 150, felt that the PIAT was outstandingly effective, singling it out for praise. Captain W.L. Lyster of 1st Battalion, The Calgary Highlanders, was fond of the PIAT's versatility, finding it 'very useful for house clearing' (Battle Experience Questionnaires, Vol. 10,450). Commenting that the PIAT had 'great blasting power, men who know how to use it, love it', Captain R.D. Bacon, of 1st Battalion, The Calgary Highlanders, believed that the No. 68 and No. 74 'Sticky Bomb' anti-tank grenades were useless; he felt the PIAT was 'so much better', noting that his men would rather use the PIAT (Battle Experience Questionnaires, Vol. 10,450). In terms of the psychological impact on the enemy, Major W.C. Allan of 1st Battalion, The West Nova Scotia Regiment, was of the opinion that 'enemy tanks did not relish the PIAT and could be forced to turn tail moderately easy'; he believed this played a pivotal role in breaking up many German counter-attacks as most of the supporting infantry 'broke except on very rare occasions' (Battle Experience Questionnaires, Vol. 10,450). This is something encountered in earlier accounts of the PIAT in action. From the responses to the questionnaires

ABOVE LEFT
Private G. Mill of 2nd Battalion, The Gloucestershire Regiment, poses with his PIAT over his shoulder, 6 March 1945; note that the butt assembly is not properly aligned. In the background, discarded on the ground against regulations, is an empty PIAT bomb carrier. (© IWM B 15267)

ABOVE RIGHT
Soldiers often complained of the PIAT's weight and invariably found innovative ways to transport it in the field. Here men of 1st Battalion, The Queen's Own Cameron Highlanders of Canada, carry a PIAT, a Sten submachine gun and a No. 4 rifle on a commandeered wheelbarrow near Oldenburg, Germany. (Library and Archives Canada, MIKAN No. 3563512)

it appears that Canadian opinion of the PIAT was overwhelmingly positive, with only three officers considering it ineffective.

The PIAT's shortcomings were generally understood, including its relatively short range. Soldiers were warned about this early in their training, with the 1944 No. 1 supplement to the manual stating on its very first page that one of the weapon's characteristics was its short range, 'of approximately 100 yards' (Projector, Infantry, Anti-Tank, Mk I, Supplement No. 1, 1944: 1). Soldiers often advanced much closer than 100yd and Sergeant James Wyndham, who fought in Italy, felt the PIAT was highly effective as an anti-tank weapon as long as the operator waited until the target approached sufficiently close to his position (IWM 20793). George Drew served with 8th Battalion, The Suffolk Regiment, and vividly remembered the PIAT's vicious recoil, but commented that it was a useful weapon in the right hands as long as a hit could be scored in the right place (IWM 28546).

Early in its service life the PIAT certainly had its shortcomings, which led to some troops forming negative opinions of the weapon. Anthony Colgan, a Universal Carrier driver with 9th Battalion, The Durham Light Infantry, remembered his uninspiring introduction to the PIAT. When an instructor shot a PIAT at a target across a small valley, he fired and missed three times in succession (IWM 21658). Many soldiers' abiding memory of the PIAT was its stout recoil, some even suggesting it could break shoulders. Unsurprisingly, the PIAT enjoyed a divisive reputation, as highlighted by Corporal Harry Martin of 7th Battalion, The Royal Welch Fusiliers. Martin was one of those who believed that the PIAT's recoil could break the user's shoulder (IWM 21105).

The reality was that injuries were often the result of user error. Unless soldiers pulled the weapon into their shoulder or if they relaxed before it had fully cycled, they were likely to be jostled and experience a kick not unlike firing a hot 12-gauge shotgun cartridge while holding the gun loosely. Bruce Coombes of 6th Battalion, The Royal Welch Fusiliers, explained that because there was a brief delay as the spigot travelled forward, the user would momentarily relax and then experience a fierce jolt (IWM 21106). With the strong recoil clearly visible and men making the mistake of not handling the weapon firmly, some new recruits, among them Eddie Clarke, were afraid of firing the weapon. Training with the PIAT in 1949 after joining 1st Battalion, The Cameronians (Scottish Rifles), Clarke watched as his fellow recruits struggled with the recoil. He later recalled that he disliked and feared the weapon, feeling that he was not fully in control of it (IWM 26579). Despite this, Clarke and other soldiers recognized the PIAT's capabilities and appreciated its war record. Jim Dunphy was one of thousands of National Servicemen who were trained to use the PIAT after the war. Like Clarke he remembered the fierce recoil, likening it to being kicked in the shoulder by a horse; he recalled welcoming the PIAT's replacement, the bazooka, which arrived in time for service in Korea (IWM 30396).

Soldiers frequently complained of the difficulty of manually cocking the PIAT. Major John Graham of 2nd Battalion, The Argyll and Sutherland Highlanders, later recalled the process. The user had to compress the

A PIAT gunner of 51st (Highland) Division, with his ammunition close at hand, awaits enemy tanks in Normandy, 9 August 1944. (© IWM B 8913)

spring, which was most readily achieved by standing up and employing the shoulder – not always feasible on the battlefield (IWM 8337).

Despite being lighter than a Boys Anti-Tank Rifle, the PIAT's weight was often a cause for complaint. An anonymous New Zealander's impressions of the PIAT, after being handed one when he reached his new unit, were recorded in the official war history of the 25th New Zealand Infantry Battalion. Like all new soldiers, he was given the 32lb PIAT to carry; by the time the soldier reached the top of a muddy slope, the weapon seemed to have doubled in weight (Puttick 1960: 549).

Lieutenant Sydney Jary, a platoon commander with 4th Battalion, The Somerset Light Infantry, felt that the PIAT paled in comparison with the anti-tank weapons used by German troops. Jary noted that the *Panzerschreck* was larger and longer-ranged than the American bazooka, while the *Panzerfaust* was highly effective and well-conceived (Kite 2014: 379). Major Graham agreed with this assessment, noting that the PIAT was very crude, and inferior to the *Panzerfaust* (IWM 8337).

Private Lionel Roebuck, serving in North-West Europe with 2nd Battalion, The East Yorkshire Regiment, felt that generally the PIAT was not received enthusiastically, with many men lacking confidence in the weapon, which seemed to offer the user only one chance of success (IWM 13584). Interestingly, another of the PIAT's detractors was Sergeant Thornton of 2nd Battalion, The Oxfordshire and Buckinghamshire Light Infantry, who had destroyed the first tank to approach Pegasus Bridge. Despite his exploits with the PIAT he maintained a rather dim view of the weapon, recalling after the war that it was inadequate as it was so short-ranged and its success relied on hitting the target with the first round because it took so long to reload (Fowler 2013: 45).

HOW EFFECTIVE WAS THE PIAT?

One of the main questions asked of the PIAT is, 'Just how effective was it?' It is impossible to put a precise figure on how many enemy vehicles were knocked out by the PIAT during the course of the war, but an analysis of German tank losses during Operation *Overlord*, between

6 June and 31 August 1944, gives us some indication of its effectiveness. According to the report (TNA WO 291/1331, drawn up by 21st Army Group's Operational Research Section), the PIAT accounted for an impressive 7 per cent of all German tanks destroyed during the initial fighting after D-Day. This outstripped even the roving Allied air patrols, which used rockets to hunt German railway traffic and vehicles from the air, claiming 6 per cent of enemy armour during the same period (French 2000: 89).

Another interesting, but hardly conclusive, method is to examine the number of medals awarded for actions involving the PIAT. In addition to the seven Victoria Crosses awarded for actions directly involving the weapon, dozens more actions were recognized with Military Medals, Distinguished Service Orders, Military Crosses and mentions in despatches.

In terms of penetration, the PIAT certainly punched above its weight. Some of the earliest penetration data from the field comes from a report written in late March 1943 by Captain F.W. Burton of the SASC. During the SASC instructional tour of Tunisia, Burton was able to gather data on the PIAT's impact on a variety of tanks including a Tiger I. The PIAT was first tested against a PzKpfw II light tank, with the report noting that it penetrated 'the thickest part of the tank', punching though a maximum of 2.8in of frontal armour (Report on Functioning of PIAT During the Instructional Tour of North Africa, 22/03/43). Petrol cans were placed in the crew positions; on inspection after firing these were 'riddled with holes … with much evidence of splash' (ibid.). The PIAT was then tested against a PzKpfw III medium tank with additional protective armour spaced 5in from the tank hull. The PIAT rounds punched through the outer layer of 0.4in-thick additional armour and then penetrated the 2.4in-thick frontal armour. One round penetrated directly through the gun mantlet and side armour, 1.6in thick and sloped at 15 degrees. Trials against a Tiger I heavy tank were also carried out, with penetration of the 3.2in-thick turret armour achieved; three rounds fired into the front hull where the armour was 4.1in thick failed to penetrate, but 'caused dents and flaking on far side of plate' (ibid.). Burton hypothesized that penetration from a PIAT round had a good chance of igniting fuel and ammunition stored inside a tank, while the 'splash' and fragments thrown from penetrated armour plate was likely to cause severe wounds to a vehicle's occupants; he was soon proved correct.

A subsequent investigation into the penetration of spaced armour plates, carried out at P&EE Shoeburyness in December 1942, found that the PIAT could be defeated by spaced plates of armour. When fired at a 0.8in-thick plate 150ft away the PIAT round failed to penetrate a second, 2in-thick, plate

Lance-Corporal J.A. Thrasher of Canada's 2nd Battalion, The Westminster Regiment (Motor), stands astride the German self-propelled gun he destroyed. He has his PIAT slung over his shoulder and a belt of machine-gun ammunition around his neck. The photograph was taken near Pontecorvo, Italy, on 26 May 1944. (Library and Archives Canada, MIKAN No. 3231053)

situated 7.7in behind it. While the PIAT rounds had no trouble penetrating the first plate, the distance between the plates dissipated the penetrating effect of the explosion, leaving just a dent on the second plate. A 2-pdr anti-tank gun, fitted with a Littlejohn squeeze-bore adaptor – a device which attached to the muzzle of a gun and increased the projectile's velocity by squeezing to create greater pressure behind it as it left the barrel – also failed to penetrate the rear plate (OB Proc. No. Q857, 07/12/42).

Within its effective range the PIAT was accurate in the hands of a well-trained soldier. Recollections from veterans frequently noted that the PIAT was a reasonably accurate weapon. Private Raymond Burdett, a National Serviceman with 1st Battalion, The Suffolk Regiment, recalled the bomb's unusual trajectory once fired, noting that it would move in a circular motion before straightening up and hitting the target (IWM 29729). Similarly, in its secondary role as a light mortar the PIAT was found to be 'extremely accurate as a low elevation mortar', according to a 1943 SASC report (OB Proc. No. AG 1,000, 15/01/43).

In February 1944, the Army Operational Research Group published a somewhat negative report on the effectiveness of the PIAT, based on field exercises; it commented that the chances of the PIAT destroying enemy tanks were slim. Tests were carried out to see how many hits could be scored against an advancing, retreating and crossing tank. It was found that the most number of hits were achieved when a tank was retreating and the least when it was advancing towards the PIAT. The AORG opined that it was 'not possible to hit any particular chosen part of the tank' while it was moving and recommended that PIAT training doctrine be re-evaluated to maximize the weapon's potential (AORG Report 164 'Effectiveness of PIAT Shooting', 1944). While interesting, the report does not necessarily correlate with the PIAT's use in the field. As we have seen, the PIAT proved to be one of the most useful anti-tank weapons during Operation *Overlord*.

A German soldier demonstrates a captured PIAT, with an early-pattern monopod, for General der Panzertruppe Adolf-Friedrich Kuntzen, commander of LXXXI. Armeekorps, in May 1944. The PIAT was a very different beast from its German contemporaries and was given the German small-arms designation Panzerabwehrwaffe 789(e). (Bundesarchiv Bild 101I-300-1862-13A Foto: Speck)

A *Panzerschreck*, courtesy of the SASC Infantry Weapons Collection Trust. Based upon the American bazooka, the *Panzerschreck* or RPzB 54 fired an 8.8cm rocket with a HEAT warhead which was reportedly capable of penetrating up to 6.3in of armour. (Author's photograph)

THE PIAT AND ITS CONTEMPORARIES

It is undeniable that the PIAT was a heavy, somewhat flawed weapon that was difficult to cock, but how did it compare to its contemporaries? One of its primary disadvantages was its weight: at 32lb unloaded, it was twice the weight of an M1 bazooka and 20lb heavier than a Panzerfaust 60. The bazooka and *Panzerschreck*, however, were both long, awkward weapons with overall lengths 15in and 20in longer than the PIAT, respectively. In terms of comparative penetration, the PIAT held its own throughout its wartime service. When it entered service in March 1943, the PIAT arguably had the best penetration of any shoulder-fired anti-tank weapon in use. It was, however, overtaken by later German and American developments.

One of the main advantages of the PIAT was its lack of back-blast. The recoilless and rocket-based weapons used by US and German troops produced large amounts of heat which could be dangerous if these weapons were used in a confined space. For example, the *Panzerfaust*, a recoilless weapon, required a 10ft area behind the operator that was clear of troops, equipment and anything that might reflect blast back on the operator such as walls or trench parapets. The back-blast could cause serious injury to anyone caught by it. By contrast, PIAT teams could fire safely from within buildings, trenches and within positions that had troops to their rear with no danger of injury. Similarly, the PIAT was also a more concealable weapon; unlike the rocket-based anti-tank weapons the PIAT created little blast and flash, and its report was similar to that of a shotgun – difficult to pinpoint in the cacophony of battle. This was first noted during field testing in Tunisia, in March 1943. A SASC report notes the weapon's 'lack of flash, muzzle blast and noise', with smoke only apparent on humid days (Report on Functioning

THE PIAT AND ITS CONTEMPORARIES						
Weapon	Service debut	Calibre	Weight (unloaded)	Length	Range	Approximate penetration
PIAT	March 1943	3.3in	32lb	39in	110yd (direct) 350yd (indirect)	4.5in
M1 rocket launcher	November 1942	2.36in	13.2lb	54in	150yd	2–3in
M9 rocket launcher	October 1943	2.36in	15.1lb	61in	150yd	4in
Panzerfaust 30	August 1943	1.8in	11lb (loaded)	41in	32yd	5.5in
Panzerfaust 60	Early 1944	2in	14.5lb (loaded)	41in	65yd	7.9in
Panzerfaust 100	September 1944	2.4in	14.5lb (loaded)	41in	110yd	9in
Panzerschreck	November 1943	3.5in	20lb (21lb with shield)	65in	164yd	6in

of PIAT, 22/03/43). The PIAT did, however, have to be fired from a supported position wherever possible, as its weight and recoil made firing while standing or kneeling difficult.

While the PIAT's spring is often mocked, it did have some advantages over the electrically ignited, battery-powered rocket launchers. The M1/M1A1 bazooka's two-cell battery proved to be unreliable in cold and wet weather, which necessitated the later move to a magneto in the M9. The PIAT's rate of fire was, in theory at least, faster than that of its contemporaries. During initial testing of the prototype, six rounds were fired within 45 seconds. A good PIAT team could certainly fire 4–5 rounds per minute, whereas the *Panzerfaust* was a single-shot, throwaway weapon and the electrically ignited *Panzerschreck* and bazooka required the No. 2 to attach wires from the bomb to contacts on the launcher. While the manual of arms for the PIAT wasn't as simple as the *Panzerfaust*'s, unless the PIAT needed to be re-cocked, the No. 2 simply had to load a new bomb. While the M1 bazooka might have needed its igniter battery to be changed while in action, however, in comparison the PIAT's cocking mechanism was a grave disadvantage when under fire. Finally, one advantage enjoyed by the PIAT but possessed by none of the other weapons was its ability to be used indirectly as a light mortar: this versatility proved to be a very useful feature.

The spigot-mortar concept can largely be seen as an evolutionary dead end, with few modern weapons using the system. One exception to this is the French Lance-grenade individuel Mle F1, in commercial production by Rheinmetall as the Fly-K Mortar: the system launches a 51mm projectile from a spigot – either a single man-portable mortar or a launcher capable of firing of a salvo of 12, similar to the Hedgehog. The marketing of the weapon leans on many of the advantages of the spigot mortar, including simplicity, the absence of muzzle flash and smoke and a relatively quiet report. The weapon is currently in service with the French Army.

ABOVE LEFT
An American private instructs two British NCOs in how to use the M1 bazooka rocket launcher in Italy, in 1943. (© IWM NA 8376)

ABOVE RIGHT
Anzio, Italy, February 1944: Captain W. Guest-Gordons, an Intelligence Officer serving with 1st Infantry Division, examines a captured *Panzerfaust*. These single-shot, recoilless weapons were inexpensive and disposable, with Nazi Germany producing over 6 million of them by the end of World War II. (Sgt Dawson/ Imperial War Museums via Getty Images)

CONCLUSION

As tank armour became ever thicker in World War II, the PIAT was unable to keep pace. A larger bomb would have required a more powerful propellant charge and a stronger, heavier spring or a longer travel for the spigot. During the PIAT's development it had already been found that soldiers were unable to fire a projector more powerful than the production PIAT without experiencing significant discomfort and a corresponding loss of accuracy (OB Proc. AG1803, 07/04/43). As a result, competing technologies, such as the rocket launchers then in use by both the United States and Germany, allowed larger rounds to be fired at higher velocities over longer ranges.

While the PIAT continued on in service after the end of World War II, it was eventually replaced by two rival weapon systems which had also been developed during the conflict. The first of these was the recoilless rifle (RCL). Britain had begun development of a recoilless system in the early 1940s, with Sir Dennis Burney and the Broadway Trust Company developing a series of designs in various calibres. None of Burney's designs was ready for full-scale production by the end of World War II, however, and it was not until the early 1950s that the 3.45in RCL and the subsequent 120mm L2 Battalion, Anti-Tank (BAT) were introduced into service. Firing a 120mm High-Explosive Squash Head (HESH) round, the BAT went through a number of iterations, culminating in the lightweight L6 WOMBAT, which entered service in the mid-1960s and became a staple anti-tank weapon of the Cold War British Army. The British Army officially declared the Projector, Infantry, Anti-Tank obsolete on 31 August 1956 (List of Changes, 31/08/56).

At platoon level, the PIAT was replaced by the Anti-Tank Rifle Grenade, No. 94 (ENERGA), developed in the late 1940s, and the American M20 'Super Bazooka' rocket launcher. The British Army had closely followed American rocket-launcher development during World War II and by the time of the Korean War the bazooka had largely replaced the PIAT with British Army front-line units. The M20 was

Two members of the Royal Canadian Electrical and Mechanical Engineers demonstrate Canada's replacement for the PIAT, the Heller anti-tank weapon, in the early 1950s. Sighting the target is Sergeant P. Decarie of Ottawa, while Sergeant W. Weekes, also of Ottawa, prepares to load the projectile. (Bettmann/Getty Images)

subsequently replaced in British service by the L14A1 (the Swedish Carl Gustav 84mm M2 recoilless rifle) and later by anti-tank guided missiles including MILAN and Javelin and other rocket and recoilless systems including the M72 LAW, LAW 80, AT4 and NLAW. Today, the PIAT is highly collectable, with deactivated examples fetching a premium, and many are on display at museums across Britain and around the world.

The PIAT represented a quintessentially British response to a deadly threat. It was a cheap, simple and effective weapon whose shortcomings were compensated for by the bravery of the men who used it in action. For many years the PIAT has been derided as a spring-loaded, half-baked idea which was lacking in comparison to its contemporaries. By combining insights from contemporary documents with the recollections of the men who used the weapon, however, it has become increasingly clear that while the PIAT was not an ideal weapon, some re-evaluation of its actual wartime accomplishments is warranted.

Ottawa, March 1988: a Canadian soldier aims a Carl Gustav recoilless rifle. The Carl Gustav was one of the weapons which replaced the PIAT; introduced in the 1950s, it remains in service at the time of writing. (Al Dunlop/ Toronto Star via Getty Images)

BIBLIOGRAPHY

Books

Balazuc, Jean (2015). *Algerian War: A Monthly Chronology May 1954–December 1962*. Paris: L'Harmattan.

Beevor, Anthony (2018). *Arnhem: The Battle for the Bridges 1944*. London: Penguin Books.

Blacker, L.V.S., ed. Barnaby Blacker (2006). *The Adventures and Inventions of Stewart Blacker*. Kindle Ed.

Churchill, Winston (2005). *The Second World War, Vol. II: Their Finest Hour*. London: Penguin Books.

Cody, Joseph Frederick (1956). *Official History of New Zealand in the Second World War, 28 Maori Battalion*, Wellington: War History Branch, Dept of Internal Affairs.

Czajkowski, Zbigniew, ed. Marek Czajkowski (2012). *Warsaw 1944: An Insurgent's Journal of the Uprising*. Barnsley: Pen & Sword.

Davies, Norman (2003). *Rising '44: The Battle for Warsaw*. New York, NY: Penguin.

Delaforce, Patrick (2014). *Marching to the Sound of Gunfire: North-West Europe 1944–1945*. Barnsley: Pen & Sword Military.

Doherty, Richard (2015). *Victory in Italy: 15th Army Group's Final Campaign 1945*. Barnsley: Pen & Sword.

Drez, Ronald (1996). *Voices of D-Day: The Story of the Allied Invasion Told by Those Who Were There*. Baton Rouge, LA: LSU Press.

Driffield, Harry (2002). 'Wartime Reminiscences of the Small Arms School Corps', in *Man At Arms: The Journal of the SASC*, Vol. 31: 35–38.

Dunphie, Christopher & Johnson, Garry (1999). *Gold Beach: Inland from King – June 1944*. Barnsley: Pen & Sword.

Foot, Michael (2006). *SOE in France: An Account of the Work of the British Special Operations Executive in France 1940–1944*. Abingdon: Routledge.

Fowler, Will (2013). *Pegasus Bridge: Bénouville D-Day 1944*. Raid 11. Oxford: Osprey.

Fraser, George MacDonald (1992). *Quartered Safe Out Here*. London: HarperCollins.

French, David (2000). *Raising Churchill's Army: The British Army and the War against Germany, 1919–1945*. Oxford: Oxford University Press.

Gilbert, Martin (1998). *Israel: A History*. New York, NY: Morrow.

Kite, Ben (2014). *Stout Hearts: The British and Canadians in Normandy 1944*. Warwick: Helion & Co.

MacRae, Stuart (2012). *Winston Churchill's Toyshop: The Inside Story of Military Intelligence (Research)*. Stroud: Amberley Publishing.

Morris, Benny (2008). *1948: The First Arab-Israeli War*. New Haven, CT: Yale University Press.

Neillands, Robin & De Normann, Roderick (2012). *D-Day 1944: Voices from Normandy*. Paris: Hachette.

Puttick, Edward (1960). *Official History of New Zealand in the Second World War, 1939–45 – 25th Battalion*. Wellington: War History Branch, Dept of Internal Affairs.

Rhodes James, Richard (1980). *Chindit*. London: John Murray Publishers.

Roy, Kaushik (2016). *Sepoys Against the Rising Sun: The Indian Army in Far East and South-East Asia, 1941–45*. Leiden: Brill.

Thornburn, Ned (1990). *The 4th KSLI in Normandy*. Shrewsbury: 4th Bn KSLI Trust.

Ware, Jonathan (2020). *Jocks, Dragons and Sospans*. Warwick: Helion & Co.

Wieviorka, Olivier (2013). *The French Resistance*. Cambridge, MA: Harvard University Press.

Other sources

<http://www.pillbox.org.uk/blog/216735/>

<https://www.benning.army.mil/Armor/eARMOR/content/issues/2011/JUL_AUG/
     ARMORJulyAug2011Web.pdf>

<https://www.tankmuseum.org/year-news/bovnews63935>

Army Operational Research Group Report No. 167, Street Fighting, 1945, <https://apps.dtic.mil/
     dtic/tr/fulltext/u2/a955123.pdf>

Infantry Training, Part VIII, Fieldcraft, Battle Drill, Section and Platoon Tactics, 1944.

Projector, Infantry, Anti-Tank, Mk I, Supplement No. 1, 1944.

Russia (British Empire Supplies), House of Commons Hansard, 10 May 1944, vol. 399 cc1918–23,
     <https://api.parliament.uk/historic-hansard/commons/1946/apr/16/russia-british-empire-
     war-assistance#S5CV0421P0_19460416_HOC_267>

Small Arms Training, Vol. 1, Pamphlet No. 5, Anti-Tank Rifle, Amendments No. 1, 1939.

Small Arms Training, Vol. 1, Pamphlet No. 5, Anti-Tank Rifle, 1942 (Canadian Army).

Small Arms Training Vol. 1, Pamphlet No. 24, Projector, Infantry, Anti-Tank (PIAT), 1943
     (Provisional).

Archival sources

Directorate of History and Heritage, Canada: Report No. 165, CMHQ

Interviews conducted by the Imperial War Museum, <http://www.iwm.co.uk/collections>

Library and Archives Canada: Record Group 24, Battle Experience Questionnaires, Vol. 10,450

The London Gazette, <http://www.thegazette.co.uk>

Nuffield College, Lord Cherwell Papers: G265; G268; G266; G267; G256; G269

Para Museum Archive: Reports on Operations [*Market-Garden*] from Major R. Lonsdale, OC
     11th Parachute Battalion, 21 October 1944, <https://www.paradata.org.uk/media/1488>

Royal Armouries Library (Former MOD Pattern Room Library): Box 612 Anti-Tank Projectors;
     Ordnance Board Proceedings 1940–45

Teesside Archives: 'ICI Billingham Report: A
     history of ICI's War Effort', ICI/
     HR/1/14938; 'ICI – Report on History
     of ICI's War Effort', ICI/BM/14/2/1;
     'PIAT Pamphlet', ICI/BM/8/11/3

The National Archives: AVIA 22/576;
     AVIA 53/43; HS4/156; HS4/158;
     HS6/624; SUPP 22/26; T161/1131/13;
     WO 106/2255; WO 171/1341;
     WO 199/191-1913; WO 201/823;
     WO 203/5216; WO 291/153

During long marches, all manner of methods for transporting the PIAT were used – everything from commandeered bikes and handcarts to folding airborne trolleys and vehicles. This PIAT man from 2nd Battalion, The Gordon Highlanders, has his PIAT hanging from a bike's handlebars, along with two bomb carriers, in April 1945. (© IWM BU 4809)